Only A Thought Away

G000057245

By

Viv Watson

Dedication

Dedicated to my Parents, Norman and Margaret Astin and to all four of my Grandparents, they are in the spirit world now, but still helping me along my spiritual path.

Acknowledgements

I am very grateful to all those who have helped me develop along my spiritual path, particularly to those people who have guided me in Awareness Classes, Development Classes and Open Circles. Mary was my first teacher who opened up a whole new insight for me into the world of spirit. Colin continued her work giving me confidence and guidance in relaying messages.

To Carol, I am for ever grateful for helping me to start platform work in the spiritualist churches and to Miriam who believed in me and supported me in this. My thanks also go to John and Maria who have been so supportive helping me initially, at Divine Services. I am very grateful too to Joan and Cecily, close friends of mine whom I have met along my journey, they have always shown a great interest in my work and have given me much encouragement along the way.

Introduction

I grew up experiencing different phenomena; such as premonitions, forebodings and seeing spirits, just as you see another person, I also had terrific telepathy with certain people and had vivid dreams about places I was about to visit.

None of my other sisters or friends seemed to have anything like this happening to them, so I often got teased, which led me to keeping quiet for several years, until I became fifteen years old.

There was more exposure in TV programmes about mediums and spirit activity by then and it seemed to be generally better accepted. My parents never forbade me to talk about these unusual happenings however, in fact, they seemed to be quite curious and listened intently. Both said that they would appear to me after they had passed and indeed, they have done, which I will explain later.

Probably my first experience was when I was two years old. Grandma Tansley lived many miles away in Birmingham, was dying of cancer. On a recent visit, I was told that she was unwell and was not allowed to sit on her knee, consequently, I picked every dandelion, buttercup and daisy in the garden during the

afternoon that day and presented them to her thinking
that it would make her feel better.

In the middle of the night, on 1ˢᵗ September 1956,
when we were all fast asleep. My mother (who I sus-
pect was a little bit psychic), was walking along a path
in her dream. Ahead, were two ladies dressed in black,
approaching her. They stopped in front of her and one
lady held out a white envelope. My mother was about
to take it, when one of we children started crying, she
promptly awoke, (many years later, she told me she
was annoyed that she didn't get to read the letter). My
mother had glanced at the clock at the time, it was 3.10
am, she then went to settle the child who was upset.

The next morning the telephone rang with news
of my grandmother's death, my poor Grandma had
passed at the precise time my **mother** had been woken
up in the middle of the night. Unfortunately, she could
not remember which of us had disturbed her dream.
Was it me? Somehow aware of my Grandma's death?
(As I wrote that last sentence a spirit orb moved across
in front of me). Or was it just a coincidence? I will leave
it up to you to decide as you read about my life and
experiences with spirit, in the following pages...

Names and places have been changed in certain
instances to give privacy and where necessary permission has been sought for any personal messages and
readings given to clients.

Contents

CHAPTER 1

My Experiences in The Early Days

My first recollection of seeing a ghost or spirit as they are often called, was when I was about six years old. I woke up in the middle of the night to see a man in the bedroom walking away from me. He was an older man wearing a long dark-coloured coat and had a bag with a long strap resting on his shoulder.

I was terrified and threw the blankets over me, not daring to look at him. Eventually, I fell asleep. I have no idea who it was, but an elderly man had lived there prior to my parents buying the house. Perhaps it was his spirit that had come back to visit.

My next encounter with a spirit was when I was about 15 years old. At the time my twin sister (of the triplets) and I spent most of our spare time working on a local farm, milking the cows and breaking-in the ponies.

On that particular day, I was training Flicker, a two-year-old filly and was standing in the field with the pony on a long reign, training her to go in circles around me. First one way and then the other. As I was doing this, I noticed the usual crowd of local children perched on the five-bar gate, watching me. There was also a dark-haired boy of about eight or nine years old, standing behind them, wearing blue jeans and a quilted blue anorak. I had never seen this boy before so he caught my attention, he stayed for several minutes not interacting with the other children, which I thought was a bit odd as the rest of them were chatting constantly to each other, jumping on and off the gate.

After I had finished the training session and was approaching the children, I could see that little boy had gone, curious about him, I asked them who their new friend was. None of them had a clue of what I was talking about and I was quite puzzled, as I felt that they could not have missed seeing him standing there.

A few days later I saw him again. I arrived alone at the farm, I found the top yard deserted, so I walked down the slight incline to the right and passed by the cowsheds entering the bottom yard. I spotted him again walking into the bottom cowshed. Strangely, he didn't glance towards me on hearing my approach, as I would have expected him to have done, instead, he continued to walk straight across my path several metres ahead. I decided that I would ask him where everybody had got to.

Seconds later, I entered the cowshed. It was quite a long one, with a dozen or more cow stalls on my left and a walkway all the way to the end on my right, I could see no signs of the boy, so thinking he was hiding, I decided to walk all the way to the end of the building checking each cowstall as I went. He was nowhere to be seen.

He could not have got passed me; I would have been aware of him. There were in fact two exits, the first one was the door to the midden at the bottom end, which he would have had a job to open and shut as everyone struggled with this stiff door. The other door was a stable door halfway down the walkway and it creaked very loudly when opened, I would have heard it.

This lad, by all accounts had just disappeared into thin air. It dawned on me that I had just seen a spirit. I wasn't scared at all, just very curious.

My third encounter of him, came whilst walking to the farm a few days later with my sister. I had told her about the strange events and as we were busy talking, he appeared again, this time several metres up the road, just about to walk around the bend. We ran forward to try and catch up with him, but as we got around the bend the place was deserted. We looked in the hedges and down the fields but there was no one. That was the last time that I saw him. I have no idea why he suddenly started appearing on the farm and why his appearances suddenly stopped.

I have seen several spirits since, not just as we see each other, but as orbs and what I call spirit energies, which are mainly either black or white streaks of light darting about. I have also seen mists in the shape of humans and animals or just white outlines, which I can see straight through.

It takes a great deal of energy for a spirit to fully manifest itself to look like you or me. Therefore, showing themselves as a mist or outline is much eas-ier for them.

Apart from seeing spirits, I experienced terrific telepathy with my identical twin in my youth. There were several instances when we were young that I knew she had hurt herself and would rush home to find her being cuddled by my Mum, after hav-ing fallen. Surprisingly, my sister never felt my pain, which I thought at the time was unfair, I not only had to endure my own pain and feelings, but also hers as well!

Another telepathic event came when we were six-teen years old. Our family toured Europe in a V.W. camper van, during the summer holidays. My father was a teacher of technical drawing at the local High School, so was on vacation for six weeks, it gave us the opportunity to set off and tour all sorts of countries.

Unfortunately, my mother had had a foreboding about this particular trip, she had heard three distinct knocks one night whilst in bed, for her this was a warn-ing that something bad was going to happen and she felt it was to do with the holiday. She decided not to say anything as a lot of money had already been paid out for insurance and for a cruise around the Mediterranean and she didn't want to cancel the holiday.

Her foreboding was right, there was a great deal that went wrong on that holiday. My father had his wallet stolen whilst in public toilets; We had a crash with a vehicle that went through a red traffic light, for-tunately not much damage was done, the engine failed on the V.W. caravanette at one point and my twin and I fell ill after swimming in the Mediterranean. Unbeknown to us at the time, sewage poured into the sea very close to the shore and we probably picked up an infection.

I pulled through, but my poor sister became quite ill. That day we were due to board the cruise ship, so it was decided that Mum and my sister would board the ship to go and see the ship's doctor. My father and eldest sister took the V.W. to the long-stay carpark and my other triplet sister and I guarded the suitcases on the quay side.

Suddenly, we could hear the wail of a siren and saw an ambulance hurtling down to the quay side stopping abruptly. I was horrified to see my Mum running behind a burly man who was carrying my sister. They disappeared into the ambulance which took off at great speed, its siren blaring once more.

We told our father on his return and were led by staff into a room, to wait for news. At around 3.05 pm, I suddenly doubled up in agony, it only lasted a few seconds and I suspected it had something to do with my poorly sister. Sure enough, she had been taken into the operating theatre at 3 o'clock and the pain I had felt was probably when the surgeon made his first Incision a few minutes later. Thankfully, she made a good recovery, but we missed the cruise as she had to stay in hospital for a full week.

Unfortunately, it wasn't the last time that I felt the surgeon's blade on my sister. Several years later there was a similar incident. I was having my coffee break at work and was sitting in a nice comfy armchair in the nurse's sitting room, when I felt tremendous abdominal pain and bent over clutching my tummy, gasping for breath. The other nurses were alarmed and asked if I was OK. I told them that I would be alright in a minute, realising that this pain had something to do with my sister again, I took note of the time. Later, I found out that she had gone into surgery for an emergency operation.

Telepathy wasn't just with my sister, whilst at university I experienced it with several people. It was like being tuned into them and I could do this better with certain people than others. One of the most memorable times was when I was going out with Mark at university.

Mark lived in a hall of residence, a good twenty-minute walk away from where I lived. There were no mobile phones in those days, only one public phone on site which was constantly in use so Mark would often just appear at my flat, at the hall of residence without prior arrangement.

I became familiar with the feeling that I got, almost like butterflies in my tummy when he was getting ready to see me. The feeling changed when he left the building, so I was aware that he was on his way then and would put the kettle on the stove, ready for a cup of coffee. He was always surprised that I knew he was coming. I could even determine if he was walking up to my place, or had received a lift, because when he got into a car the feelings would stop, (perhaps he was engaged in conversation and no longer thinking about me and the link was broken.)

If he had accepted a lift, I knew then that he would be with me in less than ten minutes. Unfortunately, my telepathy caused our break up. One day I sensed that he was getting ready to come and see me around 3 pm, the feelings stopped for an hour, I guessed that friends had dropped by and had stayed for a while, I picked up the feelings once more after that. Then, the sense changed and I knew that he had left the building, it stopped again and I realized that he had got a lift. Shortly after that he arrived.

I was eager to know if my assumptions had been correct and said to him, "You started getting ready very early didn't you, did someone drop in for coffee and who gave you a lift?"

My assumptions had been correct, he could not believe that I knew his movements in such detail, just through telepathy. He accused me of spying on him, looking through his window and no longer wished to go out with a weirdo! I was devastated, as I liked him very much, but it taught me a lesson, to keep quiet about such matters and not to put the kettle on, until my visitors had arrived!

I had different telepathic feelings for different people and so could distinguish who was on their way to see me. It at least gave me a chance to tidy up and look presentable before they arrived.

When working on the wards at the hospitals, I experienced several unusual events. Whilst I was a staff nurse on night duty on a Clinical Investigations Unit, I came across a spirit prankster. This man must have been a bit of a prankster in life and may have passed over on that ward and decided to practise his pranks on the nurses.

I had only just started working on the ward, which was split into two to accommodate the few people who had to stay overnight following a procedure. The other side of the ward was allocated to those who had had orthopaedic surgery at the Day Clinic and who weren't fit enough to go home. Two pairs of nurses were rostered to cover each side.

One night, I was checking on the patients, walking the length of the ten bedded-bay, it was quite gloomy with only the night ceiling lights on. Everyone seemed settled until I approached the last bed on the right-hand side, I could see a slim dark-haired man in his forties sitting in the bedside chair in his stripped pyjamas.

I was wondering what he was doing out of bed and glanced at the bed next to the chair, to my surprise there was someone in it. I glanced back to the chair again and the man in the stripped pyjamas had disappeared.

I didn't say anything to Cath, the nurse with whom I was working as I knew she was frightened of spirits and I didn't want to alarm her.

Helen, a nurse from the other end of the ward came to introduce herself a little later. I asked if the ward was haunted and recounted my tale. "Oh, you mean Ely, he is our resident ghost," she said and went on to say that he visited frequently. Apparently, he had done much the same thing to another nurse, who saw him enter a side room. She had gone in seconds later to see if he was alright and found him sat in the chair, she glanced at an occupied bed, just as I had done and found him gone when she looked back at the chair.

Whilst Helen was talking, the X-ray display machine which we had turned on to give us extra light began to flicker. "Stop it Ely!" Helen demanded and the flickering stopped immediately. Cath was quite unnerved by this time.

I later experienced his antics on several occasions; hearing his footsteps up the corridor or switching lights off and on. One night, I had to take a patient's blood pressure every hour. We had a machine called a Dinamap which could be wheeled to the bedside and the information came up on a lighted screen, saving us having to put the bright overhead bed light on.

As I put the cuff around the patient's arm, the over-head bedside light came on and stayed on until the very second that I finished! The patient was naturally alarmed as he had never seen me switch it on and the hand control was in its slot on the wall next to the bed.

I tried to reassure him by saying there must be something wrong with the electrics. Unfortunately, it happened again the next time I went to do his blood pressure, the patient was visibly shaken this time. Telepathically, I told Ely to stop it, as it was upsetting the patient. The light went off immediately and thank-fully he didn't do it again.

Whilst growing up I experienced another phenomenon, vivid dreams of places that I was about to visit in the next day or so, but not exactly in the same context. Let me explain: On one occasion, I was about sixteen years old. We had a couple of Bulgarian girls staying with us, they were part of a choir from Sofia, who were giving concerts at various local venues. They had a day off from performing and my Dad decided to take us all out to a museum.

A few nights beforehand, I had dreamt that I was a seven-year-old girl, living in a big manor house with my father. There was a long road leading up to the house which had a white dome supported by four pillars, at the entrance steps led up on three sides to a paved area in front of the main door. On the underside of the dome hung a bell.

In another part of my dream, I was outside waving good bye to my father who was about to set off on a hunt. He was seated on his thoroughbred horse, wearing a typical hunting outfit; a red jacket, black riding hat, jodhpurs and black boots. Beagle dogs were milling around him.

On entering the driveway to this museum in my Dad's car, I could see the familiar looking manor house in the distance and said to my father that we had been there before. He assured me that we hadn't and there was no way that I could have visited on my own, as it was quite a distance away from home.

Arriving closer, I could see the dome, the steps and pillars just as I had seen them in my dream. The only difference was, there was no bell. Had there been a bell there at one time I wondered?

We went inside, it all felt so familiar and I took my sister to the priest hole, which I knew was situated in the wall on the stairs. There it was, the little door in the wood panelling, open to show the public. Each room had the old furniture of times gone by, for me it was all so familiar, but the greatest surprise was yet to come.

When we eventually ventured down to the gift shop, we stopped to look at the postcards. I got the shock of my life, when I noticed a postcard showing the exact scene of my father setting off on a hunt, just as I had seen in my dream. I remember the hairs on the back of my neck, standing up on end. As the years went by, this type of dream became the general trend whenever I was visiting a new place.

Another time, I dreamt that I was a little girl of seven again. I entered a room, in a modern house this time. The walls were painted in a cream colour and there was a white leather settee positioned in the bay window, matching armchairs were on either side of it. Each side of the fireplace were alcoves and in each of these alcoves leaning against the wall, was an African spear about six feet long, standing next to an oval shield covered in antelope fur. Being just a child in my dream, I was attracted to them and was about to go and play with them, when I heard someone coming, so I dashed behind the sofa to hide. The dream ended.

A few days later, I was going with my sister to her boyfriend's house. We drew up in the car outside and were greeted at the door, then the lounge door was opened for us to enter. I stopped dead in my tracks, for there was the room exactly as I had seen it in my dream, the same colour scheme, the bay window with the settee and in the alcoves were the African weapons. It took my breath away.

I became quite used to "seeing" places before I visited them, but was surprised when I went to university and didn't experience anything. After all, leaving home was the biggest change in my life at that time and seemingly, I had had no previous premonition.

However, prior to leaving, I did have a reoccurring dream that I didn't connect with anything least of all going to university. It was of an eagle flying in a clear blue sky. This dream came night after night for several months before I left for uni.

I had settled into the halls of residence and three months had passed, when I came to realise the significance of this dream.

Our evening meal was served in a canteen, in a building across the road. On returning after my meal one day, I approached the main entrance to Dale Hall, where I lived. There was a canopy at the entrance, held up by steel poles. On that occasion, I happened to look up and painted underneath the canopy, was a picture of an eagle on a pale blue background. Underneath, was a painted scroll on which was written the university insignia. It had been there all the time of course, I had only just spotted it. Now, I knew the significance of my dream.

Other phenomena I experienced and that I dreaded, were forebodings. The feeling of dread and something awful about to happen, would come over me. I didn't know when it was going to come about or what the circumstances would be, I only knew that this awful feeling would remain with me until the terrible event was over.

Thankfully, I haven't had too many of these feelings of foreboding and now that my spirit Grandpa can communicate with me, he warns me verbally, so I don't have to be in the dark about what is going to happen and I can be forearmed as well as forewarned. I will mention these experiences in a later chapter.

At this point in my life, I had to contend with these dreadful forebodings. One day, my husband, myself and our ten-month-old daughter had spent the day visiting my parents at their caravan, on a campsite at Stainforth near Settle in the Yorkshire Dales. We had had a lovely day together and as we were about to set off, I suggested that I drove home. We had only had the car for four days and I wanted to get used to it.

As soon as I sat in the driver's seat, an awful dread came over me. At first, I ignored it, thinking that perhaps I was a bit nervous driving a different car, but the feeling continued. As we drove along it didn't go away. I mentioned it to my husband and he suggested that he drove, I declined, I wasn't going to be beaten by my feelings. We journeyed for several miles along the windy roads then, I steered around a corner and there immediately in front of us was a queue of cars.

I jammed on the brakes as hard as I could and breathed a sigh of relief as I had managed to stop without hitting the car in front of us.

My relief was short lived however, as there was an almighty bang seconds later as a car behind us collided with ours and we were all thrown forward. Luckily, we were strapped into our seat belts and my daughter was safely strapped into her child's seat. Fortunately, there was very little damage to our car, the other driver's car came off worse. I received a whiplash injury to my neck though, which became all too apparent the next day but apart from that, we were all OK.

As soon as the accident occurred, the feeling of foreboding evaporated. I know now that this was how my spirit Grandpa used to warn me and who knows he was probably doing his very best to minimise the destruction and injuries, at the same time. I am most grateful to him, as he is with me always, guiding me, giving me confidence and congratulating me when I have done well. I will reveal all later.

Only once did I experience anything by just holding an object, before I went on to develop my "skills". I was at a friend's flat and he opened a drawer in the sideboard of the living room to reveal a rather large old-fashioned compass. When he handed it to me, I immediately had a vision of a World War two airman's face, he was wearing a tightly fitting brown leather hat with a chin strap which was unfastened, left hanging at each side of his face. The compass in my hand started to vibrate and continued to do so for about twenty seconds. When my friend held the compass, he didn't sense anything.

At that time, I had no idea about psychometry (when mediums feel an object and can give information about the owner or past events.) My friend said that he had seen the compass in an antique shop, he liked it and so bought It, sadly he was unable to give me any history about it.

Other strange events occurred in the early days too, there were times when I could smell tobacco smoke in my bedroom.

When my husband and I got married we bought a three-bed semi-detached house in a quiet cul-de-sac. Whenever I was a bit down in the dumps, I would go to our bedroom and lay on the bed to relax. Invariably, I would smell tobacco smoke, I felt it was definitely not my imagination because it was quite a strong smell and constant, not just a faint whiff now and then. I found that these times in the bedroom with the tobacco smoke around me, brought me relaxation and peace of mind.

I assumed at the time that the smell of smoke was coming from the house next door, as we had a shared flue with them which went up through the airing cupboard, at one end of the bedroom. It was not until we moved to another property that I realised my assumption had been totally wrong.

Our next house was detached, so no shared flue. Again, I continued the habit of lying on my bed, when I thought the world was on top of me. The first time

I did this, the room filled with this distinct smell of tobacco smoke. At the time all the windows were closed, so it could not have been coming from outside. I rushed down the stairs to find my husband and urged him to come upstairs and smell the smoke.

He entered the bedroom sniffing the air and said, "I can't smell anything."

I was quite exasperated, "But the whole room is full of it."

I could not believe that he was unable to get even a slight whiff, the smell was overpowering to me. He went down stairs again, probably thinking that I was losing my mind. I settled back on the bed and it was then that I remembered that my grandfather had smoked a pipe when he was alive, in fact, this was a familiar smell. I realised that whenever the smell came, it brought me peace and calm. Finally, my little brain had worked it out. My grandfather's spirit was coming around me when I was a bit down, giving me a sense of peace, letting me know it was him by producing this familiar smell. I sometimes wonder if the spirits were giving me a taster of everything to come and at the same time, determining if I could cope with all these unusual happenings.

A few years later, unfortunately divorced by this time, I kept seeing the spirit of a young girl in the house. The first time that I saw her, it was evening, I was busy baking in the kitchen and had to walk past the open door to the hall to reach the fridge and get some butter. As I passed by the door way, I could see the figure of a girl dressed in long black clothes about to ascend the staircase, her hand was held out as if she was going to hold the banister rail, long fair hair fell in waves down her back. I was struck by her bleached white hand though. At first, I had thought it was Avril, my youngest daughter, but was puzzled by the pale colour of her skin as Avril's was quite tanned at the time.

I went out of the kitchen into the lounge by another door to see if she was still watching the television. There she was sprawled over the sofa and she said she had been there for ages.

I went back to the hallway and saw that the banister rail didn't protrude beyond the stairwell wall and knew that the girl I had seen was quite a bit shorter than my daughter. I realised that I had definitely seen a spirit.

She often came after that, sometimes I could hear her rushing up the stairs. One time, I saw what looked like a bit of her cloak blow out as she ran up the stairs. On other occasions I saw her walk out of the cloakroom across the hall and through the wall into the lounge.

I never actually saw her in the lounge, but I feel my dog, Toby did. From time to time, he would suddenly start barking at the corner of the lounge, the same place where I had seen her disappear into the wall. He would then go to that end of the room and sniff the carpet from that wall along the window wall to the other side of the room. My children often got very scared when he suddenly started barking at the wall and I dismissed it, telling them that he was barking at the burglar alarm sensor and never told them about my sightings, until we had left that house many years later.

A friend who was very sceptical when it came to the paranormal, used to mock me about it, but went into complete shock when he actually saw her one day. Dave was coming out of the cloakroom into the hall when he saw the spirit girl at the bottom of the stairs, just as I had seen her. He came slowly into the lounge, his face drained of colour and sat down in slow motion, looking absolutely bewildered.

"What on earth is the matter?" I asked.

"I've just seen that ghost." He said pointing to the hall.

He looked quite horrified and visibly shaken, it was a while before the colour came back into his cheeks. I had a quiet chuckle to myself, at least he never teased me on the subject again.

The last time I saw her it was just after midnight one night, when I woke up to see her standing in front of the window. The curtains were slightly ajar and I took her to be Avril, whom I knew had been at a party and I thought she was standing there waving someone off, as I could hear a car drawing away.

It was then that I noticed her peculiar hairstyle. Her hair was brushed back off her face into a large flat bun on the back of her head and around the bun was a neat plait. I called out to her but she disappeared in front of my eyes. I had been tired and later wondered if I had dreamt the whole thing.

The next day, I asked my daughter if she had come into my room the night before because she often did when she had been at a party, excited to tell me all about it, on that occasion however she said she had gone straight to bed.

When we moved to another house, I told my daughters about the spirit girl and Avril announced that she had often felt the presence of someone standing over her bed at night, but was too scared to look and buried herself in her duvet.

She told her friend who said she had seen her too. One day when Sue and Avril came out of school, they decided to have a race to our house, both taking different routes. Sue had arrived first and thought she could see Avril looking out of my bedroom window, watching out for her. She knocked on the door and I told her that Avril hadn't arrived home yet, but she was welcome to come in and wait for her. I remember her starting to act quite strangely, she began to falter over her words and declined the offer. Sue had realised that she had seen a spirit and I've heard that she has seen several since, whilst managing pubs.

I knew I had some sort of gift, I was also aware that there were mediums, who were able to connect with people that had passed over, I had no idea of where or how to develop further, but certainly wished that I could.

All those people out there who have experienced unusual unexplainable events, as I have and don't know where to go from here, I hope this book will give you some insight into how to understand and develop your skills. Every person has a different journey though, so yours will be completely different to mine, but I hope the following pages will give you a better understanding of what it is all about.

Chapter 2

Developing My Spiritual Awareness

It was by chance that I found a way of developing my psychic skills. I lived in Southport at the time and visited a Healing Centre every week at a hotel. Whilst there one week, I got talking to Julie, a fellow client who had come for healing. During the conversation, she said she didn't have her car, it was having some repairs done to it and she would have to wait in the rain for a bus. Naturally, I offered her a lift, as her flat was on my way home.

When we arrived, she offered me a cup of coffee, which I accepted. We got talking and she mentioned her dog that had died a few years before, as she spoke about him, I could see a white mist at the other side of the room in the shape of a small dog. She couldn't see it though. Apparently, her dog had been a white west highland terrier and had come to visit us. She said, "So, you see spirits, do you?" I told her about some of my encounters and she said, "You should start going to a spiritualist centre."

I told her that I wasn't religious and didn't really want to get involved. She assured me that the services weren't particularly religious and urged me to go with her to the next service, the following Sunday.

I am so glad I did. It opened a whole new world for me, I saw mediums working on the rostrum, giving messages to members of the congregation from their spirit friends and relatives and found it truly amazing. I was hooked and went every week from then on. They gave detailed information about events in their lives, descriptions of people, dates, names and significant places, followed by advice or endearments from these spirits. Each person acknowledged that the facts were correct. Although, very occasionally a member of the congregation couldn't take some of the information.

The spiritual church services are about an hour long. They are all quite similar in the different churches and often begin with a member of the congregation giving a healing prayer, followed by a minute of silence, to allow individuals to think about their own loved ones and friends who need healing and for any ailments that they themselves may have at the time.

This is followed by a hymn and an opening prayer in which the speaker may ask for peace and harmony around the world. After another hymn, there is a short address by the chairperson, on different topics such as the brotherhood of man, or mankind's responsibilities. Another hymn may follow, after which the speaker gives messages from the spirit world to different people in the congregation, this communication, as it is called, takes up about half of the service or more. Next, the chairperson usually reads out the notices of coming events and the speaker gives a closing prayer, the service finishes with the vesper.

At Divine Services generally held on Sundays, the speaker will talk for a short time about spiritual philosophy, words which come direct from spirit, it may be about the personal responsibility that we have for each other, helping the animals of this world or our responsibility to our planet.

I was lucky enough to receive a message on my first visit. The medium did not know me at all. He began giving me quite a few pieces of information about myself and family that were correct.

He continued to tell me that, "You could be a medium like me up here." I was totally taken aback and my lower jaw dropped in complete shock. He went on to say, "You're hiding your light under a bushel and you lack confidence."

True I do lack confidence, but his message was right, because two and a half years later I did start standing up on the rostrum giving messages to congregations, just as he said I could.

Two more mediums announced much the same thing, at other services and this encouraged me to attend the Awareness Classes. These sessions were held every Tuesday evening, 7pm until 9pm at the church.

On my first attendance, there were nineteen people present, this number varied at each class. Some of the attendees were quite advanced mediums and we ranged from those who were very inexperienced, to those who could give full messages.

We were allowed ten minutes to meditate and as I had never done this, I was given instruction to uncross my legs, rest my hands on my knees, close my eyes and let my mind go to a relaxing place. I chose to relax in a hammock, strung between two palm trees. In my vision I saw my sister, who is still alive, smiling at me, no longer in pain from the chronic illness that plagues her.

I felt someone stroking my hand and later learned it was my mother, who has passed over, she continues to do it to this day. I could also feel the presence of someone behind me. The circle leader confirmed this, she had seen the shadow of a man.

In my vision, I saw a red post office van parked by the kerb, in front of some bungalows. At the time, the vision held no significance for me, however, a few days later I was having coffee in a cafe with a friend, when I looked out of the window, a post office van had parked across the road in front of the bungalows, it was even facing the same direction as I had seen in my meditation.

During the next part of the session, we practised psychometry on an item of property from another person, such as jewellery or keys, which had only ever belonged to them. This was important, because an item that had belonged to someone else would not only hold the present owner's energies, but the prior owners too and information and messages from the item could potentially be confusing. We had secretly placed our items on the nearby table, so that no-one knew the owner of each object.

I picked up a ladies' ring and held it in my hands. Immediately, in my vision I could see a young girl, wearing a white dress, she had short blond hair. A lady with short wavy brunette hair came to stand beside her and put her arm around the little girl and as she did so, I could feel motherly love coming from her. A dog joined them and stood in front of them, but it was quite blurred and kept disappearing.

The elderly lady who identified the ring as hers, was quite matter of fact when she said that she was the little girl, she had had blond hair as a child and the lady was her mother, she remembered her wavy brunette coloured hair. She told me that they never had a dog, but had always wanted one. Mary, the circle leader, advised me that was why the dog hadn't appeared in sharp focus. I remembered this phenomenon, as it came up again on other occasions.

For the first time in my life, I was mixing with people who understood me and the experiences that I had had. I could barely sleep that night for excitement, I couldn't believe how much I was able to achieve in my first class and so my journey towards becoming a medium began.

Another exercise at the Awareness Class had me reeling with pain. We had all brought a photo of a deceased loved one concealed in an envelope. We had to feel the envelope and link in to the deceased person and give any information that came through. I was quite amazed that this was even feasible, but did manage to bring though the person's father in the photos and was able to give several bits of information about him.

When we were handing back the photos, a lady passed another envelope across my lap to the person sitting on the other side of me, as she did so I felt unbearable pain in both my hands, so intense that I didn't know what to do with them, the pain stayed with me for a minute or more before it went. I asked the lady if the person in the picture inside the envelope had suffered with painful hands. She told me that the photo was of her husband who had passed with cancer and had suffered terribly with his hands.

I didn't know at the time that if you begin to experience pain from a spirit person, firmly ask them to take it away and they will oblige.

My calling to become a spiritual healer came in a similar fashion, as it had for the mediumship, from a medium on the rostrum. A few mediums, whilst giving me messages would tell me that the spirit person with whom they were connecting was saying that I had healing hands and ought to go and embark on the healing course. Now, this could of course have been a subtle way of recruiting students, however I took note and registered for the two-year course.

Healing sessions took place at the church every Wednesday morning and there were always quite a few clients who attended. Initially, I had a teaching session on how to open my energy centres or chakras. Then, I sat and observed the qualified healers giving healing. I wasn't let loose on the public until my insurance certificate came though.

At home, I decided to practise opening my chakras. I sat quietly in my chair, my eyes closed with both feet firmly on the ground, imagining roots growing out of my feet into the earth to ground myself. I asked for protection around me, by imagining a loose veil around me. Next, I mentally opened each chakra from the root energy centre to the crown and asked for the universal energy to flood in through the crown chakra down to my palms. On doing this, my palms became quite hot. I decided to totally relax for fifteen minutes or so, to enjoy the meditation.

In the centre of my vision, I could see for the first time, an open eye, I know now, that I was seeing my third eye, or the soul's eye, as it is referred to sometimes. I began to see assorted colours swirling in turn over the eye. These colours corresponded to the colours of the chakras: red, orange, yellow, green, blue, indigo and violet. Each time the colour changed; I gave an involuntary jerk of my body.

The last colour had appeared in front of my third eye, when the telephone rang. I was momentarily startled and in a flash my eyes opened wide. At eye level, to my right-hand side, I could see a white mist, the size and shape of a five-centimetre-long feather, it hung in the air for a couple of seconds, before it vanished.

I have seen something similar many times since in different situations and have been told it is spirit energy. On this occasion, no doubt, it had something to do with the involuntary jerks that my body was making.

My friend, Julie joined me on the course and since we couldn't give healing to the public until we were insured, we practised on each other at her house. I remember that first attempt at giving healing, as it was so remarkable.

Julie was sitting on a chair, quite happy to be my guinea pig. As soon as I brought my open hands down across her ears, I could feel heat going from my palm to her right ear. I commented on this. She said, "I felt dizzy last night and wondered if I had an infection again in that ear, I was going to make an appointment with the doctor today."

I kept my hand in the same position until the heat coming from my palm stopped, Julie could not feel any sensation at the time, but did report a couple of days later that she had had no further symptoms.

A few days later, I met up with another friend called Lynda. We went for a walk together in Hesketh Park, it wasn't the nicest of days – cold and overcast, but the rain kept off. Lynda had brought bread for the ducks and we both scattered the crumbs in front of us and were besieged by lots of ducks, seagulls and a swan, all eager to have their share of the food.

I noticed a mallard duck with a poorly eye, its second eyelid was constantly moving over its sore eye. I presumed there was some sort of irritation or infection there and wondered if I could channel some healing energy. When I held out the palm of my hand in the direction of the offending eye, I felt tremendous heat issuing from it. Surprisingly, the duck stood perfectly still and stayed like that for at least a couple of minutes. A few people gathered around and commented at how still the duck was standing. They probably had no idea what I was doing.

The other ducks had all waddled off by this time, leaving this poor creature on its own, but despite this it seemed quite content. The intensity of the heat from my palm grew and grew until the end of the healing, when it began to wane and the duck calmly walked off.

It seemed unusual for the duck to stand completely still for that length of time, especially, when all its little friends had disappeared. Had it felt comfort from the heat? I do hope it made a full recovery.

These first healing sessions were very encouraging for me and I went on to qualify as a spiritual healer, experiencing even more notable events along the way.

Chapter **3**

Bartholomew

Everyone has spirit guides, whether you have seen them or not. I didn't see mine at first, it was the mediums in the circle at the Awareness Class who told me of a monk standing behind me during meditations, with the cowl of his habit drawn over his head, partially covering his face. I was aware of a presence behind me, but never saw him, at this stage.

I felt his energy behind me in one class when we were learning how to use dowsing rods. Mary, the Awareness Class leader had asked us all to bring dowsing rods to the class and to make some if we hadn't any. These can be y-shaped twigs or rods of metal which can be made from metal coat hangers. There are not so many metal coat hangers about now, but luckily, I had one and cut it into two pieces, then straightened each one before bending them at right angles at one end, with sufficient length to grip each one with a hand. In use, they are held one in each hand, gripping the handle with the rods facing forward.

Mary approached me during the class and asked if I could sense spirit energy in the room. I told her that I could feel the monk behind me. She told me to turn around and ask the rods to cross if there was in fact, a spirit there. An amazing thing happened, terrific energy or power came into both hands and the rods crossed in a flash, quicker than it was physically possible for me to do it.

Next, we stood in a circle and I have to say I felt as though I was in a class at Hogwarts, Harry Potter's school, where he was taught to become a wizard in the books by J.K. Rowling.

Unfortunately, one of the ladies had a daughter who had recently passed to the spirit world. We all felt her daughter's presence and were told to ask the rods to cross if she was present. The power came back into my hands again and my rods crossed immediately, just as before.

It had been a very memorable class, showing us the tremendous power of the spirits.

I felt this again one day, when I called upon the monk to give me calm. I was at the Healing Centre feeling completely stressed having found out that morning that my e-mail account had been hacked into and had been taken over by some unknown person.

Whilst I was receiving healing, I went into meditation and saw the monk for the first time and asked him to bring me calm, which he did in great abundance, it just washed over me, all my stress and anxiety faded away. I felt wonderful, completely relaxed and at the end of the healing session, my healer sat down in the chair opposite me and flopped back. He blew out through his mouth and beamed at me, he wasn't allowed to speak in the healing room because it would disturb others, so he just mouthed, "Thank you."

I was quite confused by this reaction, it should have been me thanking him for the healing session. When we went outside to the waiting room, he said that he had had a lovely experience, he told me that calmness had been oozing out of me and that he had been affected by it and had felt completely relaxed and trouble-free. I told him about my stressful day and my request for calm. Although, I have had several healing sessions from him before and since, he has never experienced that same feeling again.

The monk started appearing regularly during my meditations after that. At that time, I would relax and imagine myself in a hammock slung between two palm trees. I sensed when he was coming, as my hands would always go very hot. He wore a very coarse habit, tied at his waist, with a piece of thin rope and also had a chain which hung from his belt at the end of which was a crucifix

When I first attended Awareness Classes, my teacher advised me to protect myself from negative energies, I needed to imagine a wall around me and to add a mirror to deflect these energies. I was a little nervous of meditation, not knowing what I would come across, so in my wisdom, I decided that I would surround myself with an igloo-shaped barrier, to cover all angles and for even better effect, I imagined mirrors on all facets to deflect any negativity. I laugh at this now; it was so over the top.

During the next class, I was meditating in my hammock and had forgotten to surround myself with the protection. Hideous faces started to appear, I became alarmed and I ran into my "igloo," of course, it was dark inside and I couldn't hear or see anything. I came out of meditation. I think my guide was testing me for my reaction and making me realise that the igloo barrier wasn't appropriate.

The next day, a suit of armour appeared on a stand at the side of my hammock. I felt I had to put it on, so mentally got into it. I sat there for several seconds and nothing happened. I thought it was blocking my meditation and decided to abandon it. It appeared again on the stand.

I asked, "Do I have to wear it all the time?"

A voice replied, "Yes."

That is what I did for a long time in meditation, until my guide called Ramonov had other ideas. I will introduce you to him later.

I asked the monk one day, through telepathy, "What is your name."

He replied." Bartholomew."

I also asked him why he was my guide, after all, I wasn't religious. He told me that he had been drawn to my energies.

Sometimes he would come with his hood down and I could see his fair skin and sandy hair, he had the classic monk hairstyle, the top part of his head made bald.

He arrived, one day with a young boy of about six years old, I asked who the boy was, and he said that he was one of the miscarriages that I had had. (I was aware from listening to the mediums at the church, that babies who don't make it through to birth and any other baby or child that passes over, are looked after in the spirit world, often by spirit relatives. They also grow up there, but not in the same time scale as on earth).

By rights my little boy should have been thirty-four years old! He still appears however, as a six-year-old, and comes through from time to time not only to me, but to other mediums when they are giving me messages. He passed on a message to one medium that I should take a three-week holiday and rest as much as possible. The message was quite significant as I had a long-term illness at the time and was constantly exhausted.

Bartholomew also told me that the seven-year-old girl who brings me daffodils is the other miscarriage that I had. Several mediums have seen her too, including Lynda, my friend. My little spirit girl always brings me a daffodil and usually places it on my knee.

As I am more advanced in mediumship now, I see her myself during meditation, she looks a bit like Shirley Temple, with her long blonde ringlets and has told me that her name is Sophie. I hadn't chosen that name for her as I miscarried very early in my pregnancy, but she must have been given that name in the spirit world. It is fantastic to see her and know that she is happy.

My little boy, doesn't come quite as often, but he has said that he is called Adam. I treasure their visits and often think how lucky I am to be able to see them and speak to them.

During meditation one day, I asked my guide at what time did he live on the earth, 13C–14C appeared written up in my vision. He must have been born at the end of the 13th century and lived through part of the 14th century.

I was also experiencing other strange events at the time, for instance, I was sitting on a bench in the park with Lynda talking about spiritual things and just before we stood up to go home, we noticed that both of us had a downy feather laid on the ground between our feet. Both feathers were white, the same size and pointing away from us. A sign that spirits had been around us.

Something similar happened at the Awareness Class one time. We had all been sitting on our chairs in a circle during the closing prayer, afterwards several of us noticed a coin under each of two adjacent chairs. The coins had been placed very precisely, absolutely equidistant from the four legs of each chair! I feel it's marvellous what the spirit people can achieve.

Bartholomew continued to visit me in meditation and sometimes showed me a glimpse of his environment, for I saw him walking up a dusty cobbled street on one occasion with his nose in a book. Either side of him were one-storey white stone buildings, the sun was shining brightly and the buildings seemed almost fluorescent, they were so bright. (Obviously, nowhere in England). Ahead of him was a man on horseback, making his way slowly up the hill too.

During every meditation I began to see eyes; white, black and brown people's eyes, as well as animals' eyes too; those of elephants, gorillas, dogs and cats. The mediums said that the spirits were opening my eyes to the spirit world.

After a few months of seeing eyes, I started to see lips one day at the Awareness Class, a whole variety of lips; male and female, some even wore lipstick! There were also lots of animal lips too. The mediums told me that I was being prepared to give a message and in the next class, I was overjoyed to give my first message.

It wasn't brilliant as I was just a beginner, but I had heard a male voice say, "Get Well," during meditation and since I wasn't poorly, I asked who this was and I was shown a vision of Irene sitting opposite in the circle. I asked who had sent the message and heard, "Uncle Bob."

After meditating, I gave her the message. She said she was about to go into hospital for an operation, so it had been quite significant that he should come through. He wasn't in fact a true uncle, but a good friend of the family and she had always called him Uncle Bob.

The length and content of my messages improved vastly as time went on, but I will never forget that first message.

Bartholomew continued with his visits and sometimes appeared with other monks; on one occasion they were reading their prayer books and another time, they were pulling at thick ropes on a boat. He has also appeared by my hammock, with his head bowed and his hands clasped behind him, sending me healing. When he did this, I could feel a sensation of something like cobwebs on my face and my hair moved ever so slightly. I discussed this with other mediums, they agreed that healing was being given, as these were the feelings that they experienced too. Fortunately, I have learnt to self-heal now, at least to subdue minor complaints such as, headaches and painful knees. It beats popping the pills!

It was about this time that I visited Southport Little Theatre with a group of people. I had joined the local U3A (University of the Third Age) and had become a member of the theatre group.

That particular evening, I was standing at the end of the queue during the interval, waiting to order coffees, when I suddenly felt a strong hand grabbing me on my waist, trying to spin me around. I turned to find no one there. I looked up the corridor and no one was there either. It seems the theatre has a mischievous spirit. I feel they come around me because I'm aware of them and they like to be noticed.

Bartholomew visited me in my meditation the next day, some of Bartholomew's actions weren't always obvious, they seemed to be quite cryptic. He wasn't a great conversationalist and didn't always explain what

things meant. Once, I watched him swirl the water at a
lakeside with a stick, making rings in the water, which
moved for ever outwards, making bigger and bigger
circular ripples in the water. I asked him to explain,
but he left me to ponder about it and I felt he was telling me that small actions can cause big repercussions.
Very good advice at the time. I didn't see Bartholomew
again after that.

Some guides only stay with you for a brief time, to
guide you as far as they can along your spiritual path
and then another guide replaces them. This was true of
Bartholomew. I missed his visits and his quiet nature.

CHAPTER **4**

Zoran

A few weeks later after my last meeting with Bartholomew, I had arranged to go and see a medium for a reading. He was very good, telling me all about my friend who had passed over a few years previously from breast cancer. He told me about her remissions and her endless chemotherapy sessions. He accurately described her reasons for the divorce of her first husband and the personality of her second husband. He also mentioned her children.

He went on to tell me about my new guide, called Zoran, who came through to him, wearing a full suit of armour, riding on a horse. He told me that Zoran had come to protect me and said that I had seen and heard his name during meditation.

I remembered that I had indeed seen a man dressed in armour, holding a long pole with a forked-shaped metal attachment at the end of it, but had had no idea who he was. The circle leader, Mary had also seen him, but I couldn't recall having heard his name.

Zoran told the medium, that he would come again during a future meditation of mine, probably at home, and give me a message from someone in the spirit world, whom I was eager to hear from.

Zoran had arrived just at the right time, to give me protection. I had been reluctantly drawn into a situation, being pulled in all directions by two certain people. Sadly, In the end I had to finish my friendship with both of them. Zoran was there to help me to take the best actions and to say the right things.

Another medium in the circle had accurately told me about these problems too, via Jeremy, a former boss of mine, now in spirit, who had sadly passed with cancer. It was typical of him he stood no nonsense when he was here on the earth plane.

He said, "You need to keep apart from them and let them learn their own lessons". It was good advice which I took on board.

Two weeks later, I was dropping off to sleep, when I saw in a vision, a man in full armour, riding towards me on a brown horse carrying a spear. I immediately thought of Zoran. The name of "Sandra", came into my head. The very person that I wanted to hear from. Zoran spoke, saying, "She was dead, now she is alive."

Sandra, had been a friend of mine, who had committed suicide by hanging herself, a few years earlier. Her death had been a big blow to me and I missed her terribly. Naturally, I felt guilty that I didn't see it coming, if only I had known I could perhaps have helped her.

Although the above message was short, it was a great comfort to me. I felt it meant that Sandra had been so depressed that she had felt dead inside, totally worthless, otherwise she would not have left her beloved child behind. Now that she had passed over, she is rejuvenated and "alive" again in the spirit world together with all her loved ones and friends, who had gone before her.

It was such a comfort to hear these words and know that she is OK. A spirit energy has just floated passed over the key board, it is probably her spirit come to visit me. I have since been told by a medium that she is helping others who have also passed over from having taken their own lives too.

It was about this time that I visited my eldest daughter who used to live in Enfield near London. We had decided to spend the afternoon looking around Forty Hall, a very old mansion and now a museum. I needed to spend a penny and walked down a long empty corridor and turned left to find the toilets. When I entered the room there was nobody about, except that I was aware of a little spirit girl's energy and this spirit child started to play games with me when I went to wash my hands.

There were two wash handbasins side by side and the water flow from the tap was operated by an electronic sensor. I put my hands close to the sensor, but instead of the water coming out of that tap, it started to flow from the tap in the adjacent basin. I moved over to wash my hands there, the water stopped abruptly and began to run out of the other tap. I moved across again to the other tap and the same thing happened. I wasn't scared, in fact I found it was quite amusing. I realised it was the little spirit girl playing a prank.

To end her little game, I put a hand under each tap and exclaimed, "I've got ya!" Surprisingly, both taps began to flow. I washed my hands as best as I could and left the room aware of the water still flowing out of both taps. When I told my daughter, she said she would have run a mile if that had happened to her, alone in those toilets.

I was also experiencing a spirit in my house in Southport. Sometimes he would join me in the evenings whilst I was watching the TV, sitting in the armchair. I didn't actually see him but felt his presence on the sofa and could smell beer and cigarette smoke. Often, when I see or sense spirits, I can feel their personalities come through as well and I could feel that he was a lovely gentle man and felt it was the previous owner of the house just visiting occasionally, as he had loved his house and had lived there for many years.

I felt his presence behind me when I was going up the stairs to go to bed one night. I was busy decorating the hall and stairs at the time and there was no carpet laid down and as I ascended the staircase, I could hear foot fall different to mine and knew he was following me. I wasn't frightened for I had felt his presence many times by that time.

He did annoy me though a couple of times when he sat on the bed when I was in it. His weight left a dent in the mattress and twice I nearly rolled out of bed. On the third occasion I said quite firmly, "Will you stop doing that?" He must have heard because he never did it again.

My friend Lynda, saw him sitting in the conservatory one day and he told her that he loved what I had done to the garden. The man had been quite elderly when he passed over. He had moved from that house into a nursing home and had died there three months later. The garden hadn't been maintained and was quite a jungle when I moved in. He had clearly loved his garden though in earlier years, because once I had the jungle cleared, it revealed a nicely landscaped garden with many beautiful shrubs and plants.

It wasn't only the old man that visited. I often used to see an amorphous shape on the wall of the lounge above the TV It was black similar to the shape of a bat. It used to appear and creep very slowly up the wall. The first time I saw it I was a bit taken aback, but I didn't sense anything sinister about it and it never did me any harm, so I lived with it. Lynda noticed it one day too when she visited, it was confirmation that I wasn't imagining it when someone else could see it too.

I saw something similar at a service in Southport, the medium went into a trance and the spirit who had taken over her, gave messages to the congregation. All the time that she was in her trance I could see an amorphous black shape hovering over her left shoulder. It was the spirit that was connecting with her.

Soon after this, I started to attend a Development Class run by Colin, a lovely cheerful guy who was always cracking jokes and seeing the funny side of everything. I thoroughly enjoyed his classes and he has remained a friend to this day.

Colin generally took new attendees into another room to assess their mediumship abilities, after having given the rest of the class an exercise to do. I was no exception and in this quiet room, he asked me to give him a reading, I was quite nervous because I had only given short messages up to that time, but his kindly manner put me at ease straight away.

I brought through his deceased mother-in-law and gave her name and a good description of her. He asked me how she had died. She showed me her intestines and he confirmed she had had problems with her bowels. She then gave me her grandson's name.

He asked me to bring forward a man connected to her and in my vision, I could see a man standing behind this spirit lady. Colin confirmed later it was her husband and asked me to bring him forward to describe him. He was of medium build wearing a brown suit and had dark hair. Colin asked me what I felt about this man, from his energies I sensed that he was quite timid, quiet and not very assertive, which was true and Colin confirmed that he only ever wore brown suits and did indeed have dark hair.

This spirit man never said a word to me, however, but he did show me an old-fashioned Volkswagen Beetle with its classic sloping bonnet. This apparently had been his favourite car and he had indeed been a very quiet man on the earth plane.

Colin then asked me to bring forward another relative linked to the other two. A lady with short dark hair and red lipstick came through. He told me the description was very significant as she was nick-named "Snow White" when she was on the earth plane.

"Sicily", also came into my head and he declared that he was going there on holiday in the near future. He asked me to give 3 significant months which I managed and questioned me why this lady had come through. I told him that she was saying, "I wish you a Happy Birthday!" Colin had in fact celebrated his birthday very recently.

Then I saw a red post box and a large white envelope being posted, but only saw the arm of the person. "Spot on," He said, "I have just posted my divorce papers!"

I was very pleased, with my first reading even though I needed a lot of prompting. Colin said he was pleased with it too, although I should learn to ask the spirits a lot more questions, our communication with them is just like talking on a telephone. This was very good sound advice and has helped me to give much better readings and messages since.

Zoran visited me in my meditation a few days later. He rode up to me on his horse in full armour with the visor of his helmet down. I asked to see his face and he lifted the front of his helmet to reveal a black moustache and beard. I was thinking that he looked as if he was in his thirties, when the numbers 35 appeared in my vision, which I took to be his precise age.

"When were you born?" I asked. 1559 appeared in numbers in my vision.

"I was slain in battle."

I asked where and "Bedfordshire" came into my mind.

I researched the above information. Zoran would have been killed in 1594 during the period of the Anglo-Spanish war. The great Queen Elizabeth 1, was on the throne at the time. Unfortunately, I could not find any named battle in Bedfordshire that year.

I had never heard of the name Zoran, but through research, I found it originates from Denmark and means, "dawn." Perhaps, he was from Denmark or of Scandinavian decent.

In meditation not long after, I saw a man in full armour, stumbling towards me across the grassy field. I recognised him to be Zoran. In the background, buildings were on fire and there was a battle in progress in the adjoining field.

Zoran was very close to me now, he began to fall, his head falling as if through me down to the ground. In the distance, I could see another man in armour sat on his horse approaching at speed, wielding his sword bringing it crashing down onto Zoran's head. At the same time, I felt a terrific dull pain on the top of my head. (I asked spirit to take it away from me, which they did immediately). Zoran lay motionless at my feet, I had just witnessed the manner of his passing.

That was not the end of him in my meditations though, a week later he was back, using a mounting block to get onto his horse. Someone passed him his spear and he flourished it over his head and as he did so, I caught a glimpse of the horizon, crowded with dozens of houses. He cried out, "The world is your oyster!"

He was letting me know that there are lots of other opportunities out there for me. That was quite significant at the time, as I had already left the church I was attending regularly, to avoid those two people that I mentioned before and other opportunities did come my way.

This was to be the last time that I saw him. He was only with me for eight months, covering that problem period. His work was evidently accomplished, and once I had realised that I wouldn't see him again I thanked him from the bottom of my heart. It had not been an easy time for me.

Chapter 5

Hiawatha, Sojen and Blue Mountain

During a Development Class, I was paired with one of the men called Barry, who gave me a message. He said he could see in his vision, three Indians on horseback, they were telling him that they were my spirit guides.

I disagreed with him and told him Zoran was my guide, not yet aware that he wouldn't be visiting again. I had never come across three Indians at that time, of course, his message proved correct. A few days later, I saw the first of these Indians....

I was at the Healing Sanctuary at Preston Ethical Spiritualist Church and had already received healing, there was still some time left before the Sunday Divine Service was due to begin, so I sat meditating, in the church.

I found myself paddling an Indian canoe, along a river. At the other end of the boat, an Indian man appeared, facing me. He was wearing a beautiful North American Indian headdress. I could see him in quite a lot of detail, a well-built man wearing the classic buff- coloured tunic, with a pattern of differ-ent coloured beads on his chest, he wore similar buff-coloured trousers. His headdress was magnificent, with long black tipped feathers, white and fluffy at the base, tied with red binding and connected to a deco-rated band, which extended from ear to ear over his forehead. I couldn't see his face though, it was very blurred, so I couldn't make out his features.

I asked him his name, he said, "Sojen." (I have since looked this up. It is a name more common in America, than anywhere else in the world).

I asked him why he had come, he told me that he was my new guide, then disappeared. I didn't see him for a while, but after that event I always found myself in the same Indian canoe, when meditating.

A few weeks later, I was in my canoe again, but today, I had been given a very short oar to paddle with and I realised that the canoe had also shrunk dramat-ically. A different Indian was sitting at the other end this time, he had a long feather dangling low, on the right side of his head and his jet-black hair fell loosely down the sides of his tanned face.

"Why am I in such a tiny canoe?" I asked, quite puzzled.

"Because you are very small, you need to think big."

He disappeared, and my canoe grew to enor-mous proportions, the sides of which were up to my shoulders.

Prior to meditating, I was mulling over whether to purchase some property or not, however, I had decided, that it would be too much hassle and had dropped the notion. It seemed that the Indian had other ideas.

The next day, I meditated again and found myself in the canoe floating on crystal clear green water. The Indian from yesterday, appeared at the other end of the boat, as before. I noticed that he had brightly coloured beads on his buff-coloured tunic and we were moving slowly down the river, there were trees along the bank, the branches and leaves of which, hung almost into the water.

The Indian started to pluck some of these leaves and held his hand, over the side of the boat, into the water. Next, I saw him put his clay pipe to his mouth and instead of smoke coming from it, lots of bubbles emerged, floating upwards and bursting, one after the other into the air. I found it very funny, as it was totally unexpected and began to laugh. I feel that he had done this on purpose, to make me laugh as my life at this time, had been quite stressful, and I welcomed a bit of light relief.

A few days later, I was telling my friend, Cheryl about it, she informed me that there is such a thing as a soap plant. I browsed the internet and found there are many species of this plant, Philadelphus Lewisii probably fits the bill best. It comes from Western North America, where it grows in gullies and more notably along water courses. The leaves and flowers apparently lather well in cold-water. He had evidently put his hand into the water, to make the leaves soapy, then put them into his pipe.

The next day, the spirit of my faithful Border Collie dog, Toby came to visit me. I don't usually see him, just feel his presence sitting by my side, making my leg twitch, (mediums giving me messages have seen him and have confirmed this). However, on that particular day, I actually saw him when I was visiting Avril, my youngest daughter.

Avril's husband was away on business and she was convinced that someone had been trying to break in the night before, making her feel quite anxious. I advised her to ask for Toby to guard the house. She pondered this over as she went into the kitchen to make some drinks.

Toby suddenly appeared as an outline, I knew immediately that it was him, there was a white mist around the edge of his body and I could see straight through him. He was standing close to me, then he turned towards the kitchen and looked at Avril. A few seconds later, she emerged again with the drinks and he disappeared.

On my next visit, she reported that she had sensed Toby in the house and even felt him follow her up the stairs at night, however she wasn't brave enough to have him in her bedroom, as I had told her once that I could feel Toby's presence sometimes in the bedroom and could feel his actual weight against me on my bed. Each night, Avril had told him to stay outside the bedroom door. She did admit however, that he had been a source of comfort and protection whilst her husband was away.

Three weeks later, I was standing in bulrushes during meditation. Suddenly, I saw dozens of Indian canoes being paddled furiously down the river. Some canoes were carrying only one person, others had several in them and I could hear the splash of the paddles and the noise of the water, blending with the loud voices of all the men.

I asked, "Where are you going?"

They replied in unison, "To war." I looked more closely and I could see them all wearing war paint on their faces.

I asked, "With whom?"

"The Americans!" I felt I had seen a glimpse of the past.

I had another incidence of seeing visions from the past not long after. My cousin Janet had visited Graceland in America, the former home of Elvis Presley and had bought a postcard showing pictures of Graceland and had sent it to me.

A few days later I decided to link into it, thinking I might get something about my cousin as she had handled the card, however, I was aware that many other people had handled it since she had posted it, so I didn't hold out a lot of hope of receiving much significant information from it. I was pleasantly surprised!

In my vision I saw a car, it was a convertible with a material hood. The vehicle was travelling down a tree-lined road on the right-hand side. I knew then that it was not taking place in England, as we drive on the left. Then to my amazement, I noticed bright orange-coloured flames curling up from the hood.

The scene changed and I found myself standing on a pavement, I could see the vehicle parked up on the other side of the road completely engulfed in flames, which rose up high into the air. I stood watching the fire, beside the car was a pavement and a low wall with tall trees behind it. These trees had also caught fire and were burning furiously.

I was quite taken aback by this vision and knew it couldn't possibly be anything to do with my cousin because she would have told me about it. I wondered if it was something to do with Elvis, for this postcard may have picked up some of his energies whilst it was on sale in his house.

I decided to search the internet for information. It took me half of the afternoon but I found the following: In 1955 Elvis had bought his first Cadillac which was pink and apparently the car had been used to transport him and the Blue Moon Boys, (his backing group at the time), to various venues. A brake lining had failed on the journey and the car had been destroyed by fire at the kerbside in Arkansas on June 5th 1955.

I was curious whether the trees did in fact catch fire and found after much searching, that Elvis's backing group sang a song about a burning Cadillac and the trees were burning too. I was truly shocked that I could pick all this up from holding a postcard.

A week later, the Indian wearing the drooping feather visited me again. This time, he was paddling his own canoe, close behind me. I was upset to see the front end of his boat suddenly upturn straight over his head and land upside down in the water. I scanned the water to try and find him, he was nowhere to be seen. The next minute though, he was sitting at the other end of my canoe and I asked him, "Is that how you died?"

He told me that his boat had struck a rock and had turned over, he had fallen out and had been knocked unconscious by another rock and had drowned. I asked who he was. He said, "I am Sojen's brother, Blue Mountain." When I enquired when he died, the numbers 1843 came into my vision.

I went on-line again and found that there is a stretch of mountains called the Blue Ridge Mountains in the mid-west of America. This could be the mountain range after which he was named. There were many Indian tribes on both sides of the mountain, but by 1843, the Indians lived on reservations. There were only two main tribes left.

A couple of weeks later, Sojen appeared again in my canoe. I asked him what his chief's name was he replied, "Sitting Bull." He went on to say," You are good at this, you will do very well." I presumed he was talking about my clairvoyance and not my paddling skills!

The next day when I attended the Development Class, Sojen said, "I have come to help you."

He did as he promised. That day, we were exploring transfiguration, when spirit over shadows someone. Colin had brought a cabinet (a tanning tent really), for someone to sit in, it was lit by a red light to attract the spirits. We all took turns to sit in it keeping very still, our eyes closed with both hands upon our laps. The rest of the group had to detect any overshadowing of the face by different spirits.

I had never done this before, so was delighted to see what everyone else was seeing. We saw a man wearing a tall brimmed hat with goat-type beard and an old woman with short grey hair wearing spectacles, even though the person whom she was overshadowing, did not have glasses on. Other spirits looked as though they were mouthing something. We could also see the eyes of another spirit moving. It wasn't always confined to the face either, the hands of the sitters changed too, some spirits had arthritic-looking hands. It was an eye-opening session.

I was still living in Southport during this period and many spiritual phenomena were happening not just in my meditations.... I was sunbathing on a mat on my lawn one day, the sun was quite hot, when I heard heavy footfall, as if someone was trudging along in boots and there was also a distinct clinking sound. It was then that I noticed a spirit man walking with dogged determination, a metre or so in front of me.

It seemed as if it was hard-going underfoot for him, probably muddy. I looked up and saw long black boots, tight white trousers and a red jacket. He was wearing white bands from shoulder to waist on each side. Unfortunately, he disappeared before my gaze reached his head.

I lived in an area called Marshside, so it wasn't difficult to assume that the land was probably quite boggy during his time and this was why I had heard the heavy trudging noise, as he walked.

A couple of weeks later, I was visiting a museum and saw a picture of a soldier in that same uniform. I told Meryl, my sister who was with me, about my experience in my back garden. The museum attendant must have overheard and asked me to go over to his computer, so that he could try to find out more information about the uniform.

He found a website showing pictures of it, worn during the Boer War in South Africa in 1899 to 1902.

Perhaps my spirit soldier was re-enacting returning home on leave from the Boer War. His route had come from the southwest, where a mile or so away would have been the sea. Southport had been quite a busy port at one time, the museum attendant explained and his ship could have docked there. Unfortunately, the coast is quite silted up now and it's quite a long walk across the sand to even find the sea, when the tide is out.

I never saw the soldier again.

Less than a week went by and it was Blue Mountain's turn to visit me during my meditation. He was standing next to me on a short grassy plain. I studied his face. It was full of deep wrinkles and looked quite weather beaten. (I feel he is with me as I write this, as a spirit energy just momentarily appeared at my side).

He was pointing at a range of mountains, with snow on the peaks, telling me they were the Blue Ridge Mountains. I asked him if he had lived, north, south, east or west of them. He replied, "On the westside, in a reservation." I remarked that it would have been lovely, living so close to nature, he said, "It was very spiritual."

I asked where Sojen was, and found myself in the Indian canoe, with Sojen sat at the other end. The river today was flowing very rapidly, and the canoe was bobbing up and down quite energetically. I commented on this. He said, "Your life is up and down." And it was, very much so during this period. We talked for a little longer, about personal things in my life.

Just over a week went by and Sojen was back with me in my meditation, appearing in the Indian canoe paddling the boat himself. Instead of me being at the other end of the boat, there appeared a replica of the conservatory chair that I was sitting on at the time. The chair in my vision had a badger laid upon it. I was quite bemused and asked, why the badger was there instead of me. He replied, "The badger is sacred."

This didn't mean anything to me, so I researched the American Indian meaning of badger. The article said many things about badgers, but the fact about badgers being highly confident seemed to stand out of the page for me.

Colin, my teacher at the Development Class, had recently made a cheeky comment, referring to me, about my lack of confidence. He remarked, that during his time as a teacher he had come across many people with bags of confidence, but who could not give much evidence, when giving spirit messages. However, he went on to say, that he had never come across anyone with lots of evidence and no confidence! This was true of me at that time, I had very little confidence in my abilities.

Sojen was trying to give me that confidence, by sending me a badger. I also received a gift of an ornamental badger, from my daughter soon after this. She was totally unaware of the badger in my canoe and the comments I had received from Colin. One might say this was a coincidence, but spiritualists say there are no coincidences and it is the spirits that orchestrate these things.

The next day during meditation, I politely thanked Sojen for giving me the badger. I asked him if he would like me to call him Sojen or Chief Sitting Bull, he replied, "Sitting Bull."

A different Indian joined me in my canoe, three days later. He had two distinct feathers sticking up on the back of his head. They were white at the bases, tipped in a deep red colour and he told me that his name was Hiawatha.

I wondered if this was the famous Hiawatha and once again searched the internet. I was excited to find pictures of him, with the red tipped feathers, just as I had seen the Indian wearing in my meditation. I also found an image of him immortalised in a marble statue with two similar feathers on his head and there were other pictures of him wearing a full Indian Chief head-dress of eagle feathers too.

He was a chief around 1450 of the Onondaga tribe. Hiawatha was said to have set up what became known as the Iroquois Confederacy, in which five tribes joined together.

I wondered if this was the same man that I saw in my vision, either way, I had seen three Indians, all pre-dicted by Barry during the Development Class.

Four days later, I was paddling my canoe and Sitting Bull was with me. I looked down at my right arm and noticed a bracelet made of blue beads, worked in three connected strands. I also saw that I was wear-ing a North American Indian ladies' tunic, decorated with beads and I asked why I was dressed like this. He replied, "You were an Indian in a previous life."

I have always had an affinity with nature and ani-mals and watching TV as a child, I had a fascination for the way in which the Indians lived, being self-suf-ficient and so close to nature.

Sitting Bull, always refers to me as, "my child", when he speaks to me. He is very kind, but has an air of authority and aloofness about him. On one occasion, during a meditation, I was holding a very long oar in my hand, puzzled, I asked him, "Why?"

"Because you are thinking big, my child"

Prior to meditation, I had been thinking again about buying property, possibly an apartment in France and letting it out to holiday-makers. This didn't ever materialise, however, as I eventually bought a house to-let, in England instead.

Sitting Bull, was also very caring and had a good sense of humour. One time when I was a bit low, a chimpanzee dressed in his clothes, sat at the end of the canoe. It was so unexpected, it made me laugh.

A few days later, he came pointing at the sun, saying, "Warmth." Then, plucked a white flower from the bank of the river and gave it to me with the words, "Have no fear".

The white colour of the flower, signifies peace to me. The words peace and warmth became very significant that evening, when someone apologised for wrongly accusing me of something. She had recently found out that I was completely innocent of telling tales and apologised profusely. We had several hugs, I felt the warmth of her good nature again and was at peace, no longer angry at the injustice of being put down for something that I had not done.

The next day, Sitting Bull joined me again and shot a black panther with his bow and arrow, without any explanation. After meditation, I was back to the computer, looking up the meaning of "Panther". It has several meanings, but the first one that stood out for me was that black panthers stand for evil and wrong doing. He had shot it. It represented that person's wrong doing, blaming me when I was innocent, it was all over with now. I was completely exonerated

Whilst on holiday in France, that year, I meditated regularly as I usually did. Hiawatha came, wishing me a good holiday. He put his hand in the river and started pulling out fish and throwing them at me, to make me laugh. A little later after meditating, a black cat walked across in front of me on the terrace, where I was sun-bathing. I took it to mean a sign of good luck.

During another meditation that holiday, Sitting Bull gave me a doll with a dummy in its mouth and not long afterwards, one of my six nieces, announced that she was pregnant and in time gave birth to a healthy baby boy.

I felt such love from these three Indians over their concerns for me and their wish to make me happy and to overcome my problems. This was shown again one day when in my canoe, I was baffled to receive a broom, instead of a paddle. "A new broom sweeps clean," came to mind.

There had been changes in my life. I had moved away from a former friend, who had been sending me upsetting texts. I had asked spirit to help me to get over this. So, I had to laugh when I saw the bottom part of the broom change into a rubber glove, which had been blown up to look like a hand. They were literally giving me a hand to help me. The hand disappeared from the end of the broom handle, to be replaced by a pink heart. They were sending me love, for which I was truly grateful.

Spirit have often given me information cryptically, I can usually understand it's meaning, but when I can't, and there is no explanation given by them, I have had to resort to research on the computer. They sometimes also gave me animals, in my meditations. On one occasion, a big brown bear was sitting in the canoe with me, I wasn't frightened because, it reached forward and gave me a bunch of daffodils! Strange things happen in meditation.

Daffodils, signify a new beginning in Spring and it was the following Spring that I gave my first private reading and brown bears to the North American Indians signify strength and courage, something, I am always grateful for.

I often saw the Indians going about their daily business and one time, I saw Hiawatha digging a grave, to bury a dead antelope, which had a fine set of antlers.

I said, "I thought you usually ate them."

He replied, "We bury them, if we find them dead."

It makes sense, an animal which has been dead for a while, although it may look OK, could be poisonous from decomposition.

The Indians are not the only people to visit me in my meditations, there are my spirit relatives, especially my Grandpa Tansley and my parents, who I will write about later.

However, a person whom I didn't know joined me in my canoe. I found myself sitting there with a small ring of flowers around my head. I could see the flowers, because on this occasion, although I knew it was me in the boat, I was watching the scene from a short distance away. At the other end of the canoe, was a WW2 airman, wearing a leather cap and goggles. He was standing up, holding a very long paddle.

He said, "Good Luck with your mediumship."

I asked him his name, he replied, "Walter Simmons."

He went on to tell me that I knew him in a previous life. I thanked him, and he was gone. I am extremely grateful to all these spirits who are taking an interest in the development of my mediumship.

A Viking once appeared. His name was Alfred, he was holding a long oar too, indicating, I was doing well. He told me that he had not been a relative, but had come as he had been drawn to my energies. Another lady in the circle had seen a similar man with the same name, in her meditation too.

Quite often, there seems to be links to each other, during meditation. For instance, three of us once, were linked with our experiences. I could smell wood smoke. The lady next to me, felt as though she should warm her hands and feet by a fire in front of her. The person next to her, announced that she was sitting by a wood fire having a chat with an Indian, during her meditation.

On another occasion, several of us were at the fun fair whilst we meditated. A man was on the dodgems, which was significant as he was having to dodge certain things in his life at the time. Another person was eating candy floss, probably needing a bit of sweetness in her life and I was going down a Helter Skelter. My life was spiralling downwards a bit at the time.

Sitting Bull continued to visit me frequently. I wasn't particularly looking forward to Christmas in 2015 because Christmas day was going to be a bit lonely. As I went into meditation at the end of November, I found myself standing on a bank looking across the river at an empty Indian canoe. I asked why it was empty. Sitting Bull said, "Because you are empty."

Next minute, I found myself in the canoe, with Sitting Bull trying to paddle up-hill! After that we were on the level, before going down a waterfall horizontally. I could hear myself shouting, "Wheeeeee." It was so exhilarating. Sitting Bull told me, "Life has its ups and downs." It made me realise that my life has not been too bad really, compared to other people and so I told him that I had done better than most. He agreed.

Another time I was feeling a little fraught, once again my guides were there to calm me. Sitting Bull, Blue Mountain and Hiawatha appeared in turn, in the boat. Surprisingly, this time it was a rowing boat and each one, as they materialised took the oars and began to row.

We stopped at a steep bank, where the three of them assisted me onto the shore. After a short walk, we came to a magnificent snow-capped mountain. It was so majestic, it took my breath away. I stood there totally in awe of it and found it had a truly calming effect on me.

Sitting Bull had been there for me again when I was feeling unsettled about a different class that I was attending. Colin had left the Development Class, I was devastated as I loved his sessions and felt I had progressed well with my mediumship. Someone else had started another class. There were a lot of absolute beginners in that class, who had a great many questions to ask about spirit and consequently not much work was being done. I was beginning to feel that it was a waste of time for me.

Once again Sitting Bull was in the canoe with me. Both of us with paddles, paddling the boat. He took his paddle out of the water and stood it up on end in front of him, his hands resting on the top of it. He said, "Had enough of this, sometimes you need a break."

I felt that he was indirectly telling me to take a break from the class. As Christmas was almost upon us, it was an ideal time for a couple of weeks away from it. In fact, I never went back there and joined a class elsewhere.

Sitting Bull, was sent to me, to cheer me up and guide me through quite a turbulent time in my life, as lots of other things were going on as well.

Before Christmas, he was there again, in the canoe as usual. He started pulling large fish out of the water and throwing them playfully at me. Gradually, a pile of them accumulated on my lap. "Lighten up, you're too serious," he said.

I started throwing them back at him, we were laughing. Then, we each held a fish by its tail and started slapping each other with them. We were still laughing when a crow flew out of my mouth and landed on a branch of a nearby tree.

Some tribes believed that the crow was able to talk and was considered the wisest of birds. I'm not quite sure why I was given it, unless he was trying to give me wisdom.

Next, an artist appeared in the canoe, he wore a typical artist's smock and cap and had a pointed white beard. At that time, I had just joined an art class for beginners and he told me, "You will do well with your painting." He was painting an impressionist-type painting of a lake with twisted leafless trees around it. The artist put his brush down and picked up another painting which he handed to me, it was a lovely picture of a brilliant sunset full of oranges and reds, casting its bright light on the sea. I thanked him.

The colour orange, for me means upliftment and red is for love and strength. In my case I felt I needed mental strength.

Then, I saw a lady tying a bow, using gold ribbon edged with silver. She placed the finished bow on a Christmas wreath, just like one that I had recently made. The bow was quite significant as I am hopeless at tying them and had to resort to watching a demonstration on You-Tube. She must have been with me when I was struggling to tie the bow, spirit rarely miss anything, they are often around us.

In another meditation, I found myself walking towards Santa, when I came around to the front of him, he took out a book from the pile of presents on the floor. The book was entitled "Wild in the Wilderness." It had quite an old-fashioned cover of green and gold, in a sort of Celtic interlaced loop pattern and the title of the book itself was written on a dark square, in the middle of the cover.

I thanked Santa and was pleased to have received so many presents from the spirit world, they are so kind. I have tried to see if there is such a book as "Wild in the Wilderness," but have had no luck in finding it. Perhaps it's a book I have yet to write.

My experiences during meditation have taught me a great deal and I have realised that contentment comes from within. I need to accept what happens in my life, instead of fighting against problems, as everything that happens is meant to be.

Three days later, Sitting Bull was with me again in the canoe. He stood up and changed into John, the farmer for whom I had worked for in my spare time, from the age of ten to eighteen. He was in his seventies when I knew him and went on to live into his nineties. He was a tall thin wiry sort of a man with a weather-beaten face and always wore a cap.

I was delighted to see him and when I stood up to greet him, we started dancing. I was twirling round and round, he didn't speak, but stopped me and pointed to a blackboard. There chalked upon it were the words, "Thank you." I felt quite emotional for I knew that he was thanking me for all the hard work I had put in on the farm during those eight years. It had been a such pleasure for me though, looking after the horses, milking the cows and driving tractors during the hay-making season.

Hiawatha appeared at the other end of the canoe. The boat started to spin round and round, causing the water to make a funnel, similar to water spinning down a plug hole. He told me not to be afraid. The canoe spun down into the funnel of water, we went down and down. At the end, I could see the brightest light that I had ever seen. We didn't get any nearer, but seeing this bright light brought a sense of calmness and happiness to me. It was amazing, and I wondered if I had seen a glimpse of the spirit world.

Little did I know that I would see this light again, many times in fact and would fuse with it. I will explain later. I think Hiawatha on that occasion was testing me to see my reaction.

Not long after this, Sitting Bull took me to an island of palm trees and there, strung between two palm trees was my hammock. The one that I used to be in, when I first used to meditate. I laid in it, feeling the familiarity of it.

Bartholomew, the monk who had been my first guide appeared. We exchanged greetings. "Everything will be OK," he said.

Then, I found myself walking up a flight of stone steps into a tower and was bathed in bright orange light. I began to dance and as I did so, my clothes changed into a long floaty orange dress. I felt completely uplifted and happy, my troubles floated away. The orange became flames and I vanished.

After Christmas, I was back in my canoe with an Indian sitting opposite me, whom I had never seen before. He was wrapped in a blanket and didn't speak.

He slowly cast aside the blanket, to reveal a baby wearing a dress. He handed the child to me and as he did so, it changed into a doll.

I have also had another similar experience about a baby. This was a few weeks earlier and as I had looked up into the sky, the sun had become extremely bright. Through the brightness had come a baby floating down into my arms. When it had settled into my arms, it too had changed into a doll, just as this one had done.

At the time one of my nieces was expecting a baby and my daughter was trying for a baby, so, I wasn't sure which person this referred to. However, my niece went on to deliver a healthy baby boy and my daughter was eventually blessed with a beautiful baby girl.

Later in the same meditation, a different scene appeared, I was standing in a quadrangle of old stone buildings, in the middle of which was a square lawn. I looked down and saw that I was wearing what seemed to be an old-fashioned academic uniform.

At the time, a friend and I were thinking of visiting Oxford, a place I had never been to, but I knew it had beautiful architecture and tremendous history around it.

I googled, Oxford University and found a picture, almost the same, as I had seen in my vision, except that the lawn had no paths running through it. I also found that the uniform that I was wearing in my vision, was the actual uniform worn at the university. I was quite taken aback with the detail that I had seen, these visions that I have, never cease to surprise me.

Sitting Bull sometimes came to give me words of wisdom. He came one day holding a staff with feathers attached at the top. I asked him why he had this.

He said, "I am the boss," I agreed with him.

He continued, "You are the boss too." Puzzled, I asked him what he meant.

"You are the boss of your life, live it well."

Good advice, I think we can all take heed of this statement.

The next part of the meditation, I was standing in front of a stage, a lady peeped around the scenery, then lead Doris Stokes onto the stage. (Doris was a lovely talented medium, who has now sadly passed.) I could hear the audience clapping and my right arm began to shake. I could feel the presence of a spirit next to me. "Don't do too much." I heard a voice say.

At the time, I was actually reading, "Voices in My Ear", a book written by Doris Stokes. She mentions that she had had a stroke from which she recovered, although she was troubled with her arm shaking from time to time. I feel that she had put that on me, to let me know it was her. Her words were significant though, I was doing too much and was very exhausted, something that she was guilty of, during her life too.

The spirits are always looking out for me, for Sitting Bull came during another meditation, to give me a warning, in order to prevent me from having an accident. I was on holiday in Avignon, in the south of France at the time and as usual I was in the Indian canoe during meditation and Sitting bull had come to join me.

He said, "Be careful."

"Why?"

"In case you fall," came the reply.

I asked him, "When."

"Today!"

That day, my friend Elsie and I, visited the Roman amphitheatre in Arles. It was very stony and rough under foot and the steps were very uneven. I took extra care and informed Elsie of any dangerous spots.

We reached a viewing platform, made of wood, in the centre of which was quite a large hole with no protective barrier around it, nor any warning signs. Most people were walking around clicking their cameras, not really watching where they were walking. Thankfully, my warning from Sitting Bull had made me more cautious, I spotted it and was able to tell Elsie. Thanks to Sitting Bull, no harm came to us.

It was not only people, but also animals who came to me to give me advice during meditation. A gorilla visits occasionally and has been with me since the very early days of my development. I haven't been given a name for him, so I always refer to him as Gorilla. On that occasion we were sitting in the canoe, when we reached the land, he got out and I followed. He climbed a palm tree with ease and brought down a coconut for me. Through telepathy he asked me to do the same. I found it a tremendous struggle climbing the tree, not being as agile as him and was jubilant when I finally threw down a coconut for him.

I took this to mean that success is often gained after great determination and struggle and the moral of the story is to keep at it and not give up. I likened this to my healing and mediumship development, there seemed to be so many obstacles in my way.

The message continued a few days later, when I noticed a large wooden chest in the boat during meditation. As I opened it, I was dazzled by the bright light coming from it and could vaguely make out gold jugs and ornaments, lying there. A voice said," You will be rewarded by your efforts."

I had moved away from Southport and went to complete my healing course in Chorley. Although I had been told it would be a matter of weeks before I would qualify, my mentor, who oversaw the healing sessions was stalling with the paperwork. He gave all sorts of excuses; not having the right forms, to being too busy to sign any documents. Eventually, he ran out of excuses and I was able to qualify. He told me later, that he had delayed my qualification, as he had thought I would leave as soon as I received my certificate, as many others had done before me, but he needn't have worried because that was not the case with me.

I certainly had been rewarded for my determination.

I was very fond of Blue Mountain, Hiawatha and especially Sitting Bull, they were there for me during a turbulent time in my life and we had great fun, for which I am eternally grateful. I don't see them anymore as I have another guide.

Chapter **6**

Mum and Dad

I feel I need to devote a chapter here to my parents, who have both, especially my father, helped me along my spiritual path, since passing to the spirit world.

They met during the war, my mother was an auxiliary nurse working at Hatton Mental Hospital in Birmingham and my Dad was a Lance Corporal in the army, stationed at Budbrook Barracks, not far away. The nurses and soldiers used to arrange a get-together and a dance each week. My would-be parents danced every weekend and eventually fell in love.

After the war they married and moved to Batley in West Yorkshire, where Dad took up a teaching post at the technical college as a P.E. and technical drawing instructor, later moving to teach at the local High School for Boys. He also had a joinery and undertaker business which he operated with a friend and spent most evenings and some weekends there.

My mother was a busy housewife. First, my eldest sister, Meryl was born and two and a half years later we triplets arrived. The family literally doubled overnight and life for both my parents was quite hectic, there were no disposable nappies in those days, only Terry Towelling nappies which had to be washed and dried. There were no easy modern-day sterilisers either for the feeding bottles, glass feeding bottles had to be boiled along with the rubber teats, in order to sterilise them.

Somehow, they managed to find the energy to raise us. They were quite strict, which wasn't a bad thing and they made us very independent, we helped out with the housework, cooking and other chores from quite a young age.

My parents never discouraged me from talking about the strange things that I experienced whilst growing up. In fact, they seemed quite curious. Neither of them was particularly clairvoyant, although my father did see the spirit of his mother sitting on his bed one night soon after she had passed. My mother never actually saw any spirits, but did hear three knocks from time to time as I have mentioned before, for her it meant a foreboding and some sort of trouble lay ahead.

I remember my Mum having another of these forebodings many years later, when she was convinced that there was going to be a telephone call bringing bad news. A family member had become pregnant and it was soon after this that Mum had this feeling, although she didn't connect it with the pregnancy at the time. She hardly went out during those nine months in case that call came, of course there were no mobile phones then, just our landline phone at home. If she did go out or visit anyone, my mother would often cut it short to go back home in case the telephone rang. We all thought she was going a bit mad! Finally, the phone call did come, it was the terrible news from the hospital that the seemingly healthy baby, had suddenly passed away. My mother was so upset that she suffered a TIA (a minor stroke). I went over to care for her whilst my Dad went to visit the bereaved family. Luckily, my Mum made a full recovery.

It was probably because both parents had had some experiences like these that they were tolerant of my experiences and both said that they would appear before me after they died.

They kept their promise. My father was the first parent to sadly pass over in 1999, having had a sudden stroke one morning which took his life. Up to that time, he had been fully fit and healthy, but this was how he said he had wanted to go, passing over before my mother and not having to suffer a long lingering debilitating illness.

It was three months after he passed before he appeared to me. My dog, Toby was still alive then and I usually took him out for a walk at 6.30 am before going to work. On that particular day, I was crossing the road to the park, when I saw a man who looked very much like my father, walking on the other side of the road, however, he appeared to be about twenty years younger than I had last seen him, he had dark hair like my Dad had and was wearing a buff coloured overall, (He used to wear this type of overall to protect his clothing, whenever he was doing any joinery work). I saw this man turn up the road to where I used to live during the eighties.

Regrettably, I didn't take much notice of him as I was distracted by taking Toby's lead off and keeping my eye on the dog instead. When I did stop to think about this man though, I realised that I had never seen anyone dressed like that walking around this area at that time in the morning. I looked around again, the man had disappeared. I have never seen anyone since dressed like that, I truly felt that Dad had in fact visited me. I only wish that I had gone over to speak to him.

Since then, He leaves me little white downy feathers to let me know he is around me. The first time it happened, it was in the early hours of the morning, I had got up to use the bathroom and had realized it would have been his birthday, had he not passed over. I sang Happy Birthday to him and returned to bed. The first thing I saw when I awoke the next day was a small fluffy white feather next to me on my duvet. I don't have anything stuffed with feathers in the house and knew that he had left it there for me to find.

On another occasion, I was in the lounge busy knitting a little white cardigan for my grandson when I noticed what I thought at first was some wool fluff on the arm of the armchair. When I picked it up, I could feel something hard in the middle of it and after examining it, I realised it was the spine of a very fluffy downy feather. I put it in a small bowl on the shelving unit and continued to knit for another few hours, when again I noticed a feather on the arm of the chair,

I wasn't sure if this was another feather or the same one. When I looked inside the bowl, it was empty, I felt that my Dad had placed the feather back on the chair, to make sure I knew he was around me.

My Dad sometimes comes around me with the distinctive smell of fish and chips. He always loved eating them and often on the way back from a day trip, he would stop the car and buy us all a portion.

He came to an Awareness Class once and Mary started sniffing the air saying she could smell fish and chips. I told her it was probably my Dad. She said to me that she could see in her mind's eye, a hefty bill and was quite shocked by it. She was quite right of course; I had recently had a service and MOT carried out on my car and the bill had come to more than £600. I had been quite shocked too.

My Dad told her that I shouldn't worry as money was owed to me and it would make less of a hole in my pocket. Indeed, I was owed a substantial amount of money from various sources.

He visited me during meditation once, leading a lady down an old-fashioned staircase. I couldn't see who the lady was at first, until they both turned to face me. It was my Aunty Jean who was with him. My Dad said, "Take care," and Aunty Jean said, "God bless you," It was quite appropriate as she had been a Catholic when she was on the earth plane.

On another occasion, I found myself on a semi-circular terrace, surrounded by a balustrade of con-crete ornate pillars, topped with rectangular stones.

As I walked onto the terrace, I could see a man standing to the right-hand side of the terrace. The man turned towards me and I realised it was my father. He was dressed in a black great coat which I remembered him wearing during my childhood, together with his familiar white silk scarf tucked in at the front.

He smiled, but although he passed in his seventies, he had come looking much younger, as a 40-year-old. It was quite significant that he had turned up, as it was May 22nd again, his birthday, or would have been if he had still been with us on the earth plane. (I had sung Happy Birthday that morning again, as I do every year on his birthday.)

At this point, I became a little girl of about eight years old and worked out later that I would indeed have been that age when he was forty years old. I jumped over the stone balustrade with him and found myself going down a very wide slide at great speed into a tunnel, which twisted and turned and seemed to go on for a very long time.

Finally, I saw a brilliant white light at the end of the tunnel and we continued to slide at tremendous speed into it and seemed to fuse with the bright light.

It was then that I found myself in a tall circular stone tower, possibly thirty metres high, which had small windows without any glass. These were situated at intervals up the entire circular wall, shafts of misty light were coming through each of them, lighting up the tower and far above, I could see birds circling in flight.

My Dad was beside me raising a glass of red wine, being very jolly in his mannerisms, although I couldn't actually hear him. "Where's Mum?" I asked.

He didn't reply, but my Mum appeared seconds later, close beside me. She arrived as a 20-year-old. My Mum often likes to appear at this age, even though she passed over, when she was 86-years-old. She looked very beautiful and wore a coat with a fur collar reaching all the way around down to the first button of her coat, she didn't say anything either, but it was lovely to see them both on my Dad's birthday.

Once he came emphasizing his glass eye which he had to wear after losing his own eye in an accident during his youth, then he showed me that he had two perfect blue eyes once again. Illnesses and disabilities disappear in the spirit world, the spirit becomes whole again, but often they present themselves to us as they were before passing, in order to be recognised.

He was a bit of an impatient man and a perfectionist when he was on the earth plane and I remember him coming to me during my meditation when I had tenants at my other house not getting on with the next-door neighbour. He stood there in my vision looking quite annoyed and said, "Get those tenants out of your house." Still telling me what to do from the other side, I had to smile. They left on their own accord not long afterwards.

Dad came another time via a medium, laughing and joking and being quite light hearted, admitting that he hadn't been like this on the earth plane, he went on to say that I had not got over a passing of someone from a few years previous and must let go. It was my mother that he was talking about, who sadly had had Alzheimer's disease during her last ten years and it had been a difficult time for her. After her death, I often dwelled on her suffering, until my father gave me this message. I knew she was happy in the spirit world and realised my worrying about her last years on this earth wasn't doing me any good, nor could it be changed, it was definitely time to move on.

It's lovely how my Dad comes around me sometimes, because he makes the lights flicker and at the same time, I have felt his presence. I have sent out my thoughts to thank him for being there with me, once I have acknowledged him, the lights stop flickering.

Much further along my spiritual development when Dad visited me during meditation, he didn't always show the whole of himself, I may only see his face. On one occasion he said, "Vivien, I have something for you." (He generally called me by my full name before he passed). His voice was a bit faint, so I asked him to draw closer, which he did, his face became almost double the size of mine. I enquired what it was he had for me. He replied, "Bags of confidence."

A similar conversation happened again sometime later, I found myself at the other end of the canoe and my Dad sitting in my usual seat.

I asked, "Why are you sitting in my seat?"

"I'm paddling your canoe until you have confidence."

It was really kind of him to support me on my spiritual journey.

My Dad was the right person to give me confidence, he had been quite an extrovert and full of confidence when he was with us. He could start a conversation with anyone and he liked to give magic shows at the Sunday School that I used to attend in my youth. He was actually a member of the Magic Circle and also gave shows in Leeds, but best of all he was our very own special magician at our birthday parties. All the young party guests used to be mesmerised by his magic tricks and we thoroughly enjoyed his performances.

I can always feel him around me on the platform now when I'm giving a service. I know that he is bringing me confidence.

He showed me his house in the spirit world once. As soon as I started to meditate, I found myself looking at quite a large house, stood in its own grounds made of sandstone with white corner stones at each end of the building. My Dad had always preferred the sandstone buildings of Yorkshire to the red brick houses of Lancashire where he grew up. I walked up to the wooden gate at the end of the front garden and opened it. I could see my father busy sawing wood on a wooden trestle in front of the house, he used to use a similar one during my childhood.

"What are you doing?" I asked.

Without looking up he replied, "I'm doing some repairs."

"I thought that in the spirit world you just wished for things and they happened." Meaning there was no need to actually repair anything, thoughts alone could fix things. He explained, "Whichever way you want it." My father had been a joiner as well as a teacher as I've mentioned before and loved working with wood, so presumably, still wanted to carry on working with wood and do repairs.

My mother came holding a lamb and I could see a horse and a cow munching grass behind her, I realized they had a little farm in the spirit world. My Mum had hand reared an orphaned lamb called Molly, when she had lived with my sister on a farm after Dad's demise, so it wasn't that much of a surprise to see her holding one. She had been a city girl in her youth and it wasn't until much later in her life that she had any experience of farming.

In contrast, my father had been very much a country sort of person when he was with us on the earth plane and had helped out on a farm in his youth and had also taken an interest in the farm that my sister and I worked on during our teens. He has continued his passion it seems in the spirit world.

Having a big house, I felt was significant too. My Dad had come from a very poor cotton weaving family and had lived in a small house and later when he married and had four children, we had all lived in just a three bedroomed house. We managed of course, but I can see why he lives in a big house now.

He has advised me when I'm doing repairs and jobs around the house. I like painting and decorating and can turn my hand to putting up shelves and basic repairs. One day I was contemplating whether I had enough paint to freshen up the airing cupboard. As I stood gazing at the partially filled pot of paint, I heard my Dad say, "There is enough." I trusted his judgement and began to paint. He was right of course, there was just enough paint.

On another occasion, I had decided to decorate the hall and stairs. My daughter, Avril had given me strict instructions not to use the ladders unless she was there, in case there was an accident. I had already painted the walls as high up as I could reach with the roller and there were only a few centimetres left to do. I was reluctant to ask my daughter, Avril to keep coming over, so I asked my Dad for any ideas to avoid using the ladders. A picture of a paint brush taped to a pole came into my mind. At first, I thought it would never work, but I took my time and used it very carefully with complete success.

He gave me a similar idea when I was wanting to stain the decking a few years later. My knees are quite bad now and kneeling down to do anything can be quite painful and then there is the struggle to get up afterwards! My Dad, once again showed me a vision of a large paintbrush taped to a pole. I used his idea. It was so much easier being able to do the job standing up and the decking was stained in no time at all.

My Mum never did any decorating or repairs, she left it to my Dad. Her married life was spent being a busy housewife, she loved sewing and knitting and made all our clothes and later when we got married, she baked our wedding cakes and decorated them. Each one was so beautifully made. Mum made my wedding dress too and had to alter it the night before my wedding, as I had lost so much weight during my finals at university. Apparently, she stayed up into the early hours of the morning to finish it, I was so grateful.

Unlike my father, my mother wasn't an extrovert. She was a quiet person and more reserved. I feel I take after her. She lived until the age of eighty-six when she passed over having been ill for a long time. It was about six am when she gave her last breath, lying in her bed at my twin sister's house quite a number of miles away from me, where she had lived for ten years. Meryl, my eldest sister had phoned me to give me the bad news, it wasn't entirely unexpected, but still a shock when it did come.

I laid back on my bed, knowing that she was finally at peace and closed my eyes. I didn't fall asleep I was too upset thinking about her. Suddenly I sensed her presence in the room and I felt as if she was giving me a hug. I could smell her just as she smelled when I was a child. Intense love as I have never known before surrounded me, it was so beautiful, allowing me to fully relax, my sorrow floated away. I laid with her around

me completely immersed in her wonderful sooth-
ing love for several minutes, thinking to myself that
I would feel dreadful again when she went away. After
those unforgettable minutes, I felt her leaving, it was
as if she was peeling away from me, my Mum gradually disappeared, but that love and the tranquillity it
brought, remained with me and I fell fast asleep.

Both parents passed over before I developed my
mediumship and I was grateful to be able to see my
father after his passing and to experience my mother
around me so soon after her death.

Like my Dad, my Mum keeps me in check too.
I was knitting a waistcoat for my grandson a few years
later, when I noticed that I had dropped a stitch and it
had dropped several rows down. I have to say that I let
out a few choice expletives because I was so annoyed.
I don't normally swear, but losing the stitch meant
pulling out several rows and starting again. Just as
I let out those forbidden words a piece of ornamental
coal dropped spontaneously off the electric fire onto
the hearth. It had never happened before, I felt it was
my Mum objecting to my bad language because she
never tolerated swearing at all at home and not once
did I hear her swear either. No more coals have fallen
out of the fire since, but then I have been more careful
about what I say!

My mother seems to come around me a great deal
and a medium on the platform confirmed this, add-
ing that my mother sometimes moves things. It was
quite true for a few days before, I had been sewing up

a baby's cardigan using a big blunt ended needle, that I had put down on the coffee table for a moment and when I needed it again, it had disappeared. I searched high and low and appealed to the spirits to help me find it because I didn't have another one.

When I looked back at the coffee table again there was another blunt-ended needle, this one was quite different though, for it had a slightly irregular eye. I used that one instead and when I had finished and was tidying up for the day, I found my original needle. Now I have two! The needle with the irregular eye must have been an apport which had materialised from the spirit world.

I can often feel my Mum stroke my left hand or cheek, sometimes she comes around to give me comfort and I can actually smell the Pond's cream she used to use on her face. It is wonderful to know that she is there.

One Mother's Day she was there again sending her love. The medium on the rostrum said I was blessed that so many spirits love me. She told me there was a whole queue of spirits at the side of her, these youngsters had been babies who had died before reaching the earth plane (miscarriages) and premature babies who passed on delivery, they were children now growing up in the spirit world and wanted to thank me for looking after their mothers, they had each brought me a daffodil. I was overwhelmed that they had all come to visit me, I had worked on a gynaecological ward as a staff nurse at the beginning of my career and sadly there had been many miscarriages and premature babies who didn't survive very long.

The medium went on to say that these children had been around me during the weekend and they were singing and bringing upliftment for me. I was so overcome, it was all I could do to hold back the tears. She also mentioned that a lady who had died shortly after giving birth was there too, I did remember this lady and was thanked by her for the care I had given. It was all so very emotional but also very uplifting for me at the same time, having all those people visiting me on that special day, Mother's Day.

In the past, Mary, my Awareness Class teacher had also mentioned that there were many spirit children around me singing, on that day they were singing Ding Dong Bell. Another time, a medium in the Healing Sanctuary commented there were a lot of children around me. Some were running about and others were clambering over the healing couch. They come often it seems.

The medium on the podium continued saying that I had come along a rough road and the spirits had been with me guiding me. She said that I was at a standstill, but would move on and eventually teach.

It was true I had had a bad time, I had decided that I wanted to retire as I had a chronic illness, but didn't have much of a work's pension, so I purchased a derelict house in Southport and renovated it with all the up and down's that entails, plus the hard work of organising contractors and carrying out some of the decorating whilst still trying to hold down my part-time nursing job. After sometime the work was completed and I managed to rent it out. It gave me added income and happily I was finally able to fully retire. Indeed, at that point, I had come to a standstill, the work was finished and I was relaxing and enjoying my retirement.

Later on, however I did become more involved working for spirit and did start to teach, taking a group of people through their Spiritual Healing Certificate and starting an Awareness Class.

About a year after my mother passed over, I had an extraordinary evening. There were lots of spirit energies in the room darting about, many more than usual. I was watching TV aware of them, but I don't always link in to find who they are except on that occasion one of the energies started to do loop the loop. I had never seen that before and realised that a spirit must be desperate to communicate.

I felt it was my mother and asked her to indicated whether it was in fact her or not. The next instance the energy swooped down into my right knee and seconds later the top half of my body was thrown forward. I felt more convinced now it was her, but was not totally sure and asked her to prove it without a shadow of a doubt.

Nothing happened for the next couple of hours and I felt quite disappointed. Eventually, I switched off the television and made my way upstairs to bed. On reaching the landing, the shadow of a female suddenly appeared at the side of me. I jumped as I was not expecting it, however, I could see that this lady's height was level with my shoulder. I knew it was my mother for we had joked about her height a few months before she had passed. She had commented that she was shrinking and when she measured herself against me, her head was only up to my shoulder, we had laughed about it. Her shadow only stayed for a second or two, but I was delighted that she had come to see me.

Mum's spirit energy has done loop the loop since in my lounge, I linked in as before and she confirmed it was her. I invited her to sit next to me on the sofa to watch the TV and as I did so the left-hand side of my body became very warm, I could feel her presence and the other energies in the room disappeared.

It was not long after this, that I saw spirit energies darting about in the lounge again, whilst watching the telly. I linked in straight away and asked who they were, "Mum and Dad" came the reply in my head and then the energies disappeared.

The next morning, I came downstairs and on the way through the lounge to the kitchen, I saw what looked like a light blue coloured ball on the floor, it was only small, about the size of a small satsuma. It hadn't been there the night before and I had no idea where it had come from. On picking it up, it felt icy cold and rubbery to the touch, it looked rather like a rubber ball made up of rubber strands radiating from its centre, glued together. I wondered if it was another apport from the spirit world and felt my mother had sent it. I put it on the nest of tables and got on with preparing breakfast.

It was a few hours later before I picked it up again and was surprised to find it was no longer icy cold and rubbery, upon examining it, I found it to be a small light-blue coloured woollen pom-pom. I didn't have any pom-poms in the house and was convinced that my Mum had left it on the floor that morning, for me to find, after all I couldn't miss it, it was directly in my path on the way to the kitchen, where I make a bee-line every day on going downstairs.

I was very grateful to have received that gift and the next time I had a reading from a medium, I took it along. He confirmed it was from my mother and he could feel the love coming from it. Needless to say, I still have it.

My Mum also comes through during my meditations sometimes and I remember her appearing as a thirty-year-old riding a bike. I said to her, "You couldn't ride a bike," because I knew she had never learnt to ride a bike when she was on the earth plane. "I can now!" She replied. (It seems that people in the spirit world learn to do new things. I've seen my Dad playing a guitar, he had never played one when he was here.) I asked her if she had learnt to ride a horse, something else she had never done. She said, "I don't want to." Swimming had been her favourite sport and she left me with a vision of her swimming at the swimming baths.

It reminded me of a time when I had been swimming at the swimming baths after her passing and had invited her to join me. All of a sudden, I could feel myself being lifted in the water and propelled forward without any effort at all from me. Mum was letting me know that she had come to join me.

A few months later, I saw another energy darting around my lounge. I linked in, it was my mother again, she said she would be coming with me to my Development Class that night and what's more, she said that she would be coming in my car.

I don't usually allow spirits in my car whilst I'm driving as I find them quite distracting. I had three spirit ladies sitting on the back seat once, I could smell their perfume and hear them talking, although I couldn't make out exactly what they were saying. I found myself constantly looking in my mirror to see if I could see them, not entirely concentrating on my driving, I asked them to go and they obliged. Therefore, I told my Mum, she could come in the car, but not to show herself. I set off, it was a terribly windy night and I had a job to keep the car steady, it was being continually buffeted by the wind. Consequently, I was adjusting the steering wheel constantly in an effort to stay in lane.

On arrival at the spiritualist church, I decided to purchase a small crystal ball, I could sense my Mum around me and knew that she had come to help me find the right one. I was drawn to a particular crystal ball and bought it without hesitation.

The class started and after the opening prayer and meditation, I was paired with Jeremy who had arrived late. He brought through a rounded lady wearing a white nightie, who had suffered from Alzheimer's disease before she passed. I knew it was my Mum. He told me that she had been sitting in the back of my car on the journey to the class and mentioned the steering wheel was juddering quite a bit. He also said that she wanted me to light my rock salt candle whenever I used my crystal ball.

Mum had evidently wanted to prove that she was in my car on the way to the class and the fact that she was sitting on the back seat was quite significant, because she was a bit of a nervous passenger in a car and preferred to sit at the back. Jeremy had arrived late so never saw me purchase the crystal ball. Mum also told him that I would see pictures and little movies in my crystal ball and I have done, but I don't tend to use it now, preferring to give readings and messages without using any "tools."

I feel privileged and so lucky to still have my parents around me even though they have passed to the spirit world, I'm sure they will continue to visit me especially when I need their help or advice.

CHAPTER 7

Ramonov

My next meditation was very memorable and quite scary at the time.

As I went into meditation, my Grandpa Tansley was with me, tightening my throat as he usually does, when he is around me. (After the meditation, I realised he had come to be with me, to give me reassurance).

I found myself in the Indian canoe once more. There was an Indian wearing a headdress sat at the other end of the boat and I automatically assumed it was Sitting Bull, although strangely, I couldn't see his face. He had dozens of small birds perched all over him.

I asked him, "why?"

He answered, good naturedly, "They like me," then, he shooed them away.

I said, "Welcome, Sitting Bull."

He replied in quite a commanding voice, "I am not Sitting Bull, I am Ramonov, I am going to be your new spirit guide."

I was full of confusion and a little dread, wondering if I had picked up a negative energy. I thought my imagination was running away with me for Ramonov was Doris Stokes' guide when she was alive, only he was a Tibetan monk and not a North American Indian.

At the time, I was reading another one of her books, was I losing it, or was this the link that had brought Ramonov through, but in the guise of a North American Indian? Or was he a completely different person with the same name?

I asked him to pinch my left ear if it was true. I felt nothing on my left ear, but my left knee became excruciatingly painful. I asked him to take the pain away, which he did instantly. I relaxed a bit, he was obviously a good spirit, as dark spirits presumably are not that obliging!

I wasn't sure if he had come as another guide, to join my three Indians, or if he was going to work with me alone. I questioned him on this, without any reply, so I called for Sitting Bull, Blue Mountain and Hiawatha, they came at once.

To my utter amazement and horror, I could see the out-line of a face, blowing a ferocious wind, which sent all three of them somersaulting backwards, bumping into each other as they went, tumbling down the side of the hill. Eventually, all three of them disappeared out of sight.

Ramonov's energy seemed extremely more powerful than these other Indian guides. I was quite unnerved at losing them in this way and still had my doubts, whether this spirit had good intentions.

Ramonov drew up a large carved wooden chair and sat down. All I could see was him in the chair, there was no background as such, just a bland grey colour.

I felt his powerful energy again, nothing like I had ever experienced before. His presence had great authority. He wore a magnificent headdress although I couldn't see his face, that area was blank too, similar to the background behind him.

Both my knees became very painful, I asked him if this was his sign that he was present. He didn't answer, so I requested him to take the pain away.

He said, "I will do your bidding," the pain disappeared in a flash. "Now we shall begin..."

I interrupted, "I would like to be involved in finding missing persons."

In a booming voice, he replied, "It is not for you to decide."

I was quite frightened of him I have to admit and decided to ask him what he wanted me to do. He said very sternly, "Be quiet and still."

He disappeared at this point and I was quite thankful to see my Mum sitting on a bench in a beautiful garden, she appeared very young, probably in her twenties. I went up to join her and asked why she had come as a young woman. She said, she liked to be that way. We both gave each other a loving hug.

I asked for my Dad to come. At first, I could only see his face, he was acting quite silly, pulling funny faces before giving his familiar smile. He held up a tie, something quite memorable which reminded me of his last visit to my house, I thought he was going to do the knot trick.

Dad as I've mentioned before had been a magician during his life here and on his last visit, before his sudden death, he had shown me how to put a seemingly complicated knot into a tie, which became completely undone, when the tie was shaken. Today however, he just placed the tie over the back of the seat. I had forgotten how to do the trick and asked him to show me again. "Another time," he answered dismissively.

I thanked everyone for coming, I was more at ease now and as I thanked my three Indian guides, I could see them calmly riding on their horses down a hill. They didn't look back, I was so glad though, that they were OK.

At first, after this unnerving meditation, I decided that I was never going to meditate again. I was going to give up mediumship altogether, as I didn't know what I was getting myself into. However, upon reflection, I came to realise that Ramonov was not a dark spirit at all, otherwise he would not have taken my pain away, on those two occasions. At the time, I was very afraid and was probably sitting quite rigidly, bringing the discomfort on myself.

I decided that although he was very powerful and came across as quite authoritative, he had a caring side, because he had left me with my parents after our meeting, in order for them to give me comfort. I finally reached the conclusion, that he was indeed my new spirit guide and I would try to look forward to working with him.

I am very glad I did, as my development came on in leaps and bounds.

Talking to several other mediums, I have found that not all of them experience anything like this during their meditations. Some excellent mediums never see their guides, others see them but are not shown their faces. We all develop in our own special way.

When I made notes about this event originally, my Grandpa was with me, tightening my throat and I saw a spirit energy float across the table. My Grandpa had been with me from the beginning of that meditation and is always there when I need reassurance. I know now, that he would never let me come to any harm.

The next day, I was a little apprehensive about going into meditation again, as you can imagine, but Grandpa came around me for reassurance again and as he did so I could feel the familiar tightening of my throat, that he gives me.

I found myself in the Indian canoe, once more. There at the other end of the boat was an Indian in full headdress, wearing beige trousers and a tunic top. I couldn't see his face though. I said, "Hello, is it Sitting Bull or Ram......

Before I could finish saying Ramonov, he interrupted, "Ramonov," he boomed.

There was a pause and he proceeded to say, "I need to talk to you."

"I'm listening. Go ahead." I replied.

He continued, "The world is a wonderful place."

It was significant that he should mention this, as recently; I had been hating the world or more precisely certain people in it. Those who caused wars, terrorism and pollution and all the suffering that it brings, it had left me feeling very depressed at the state of our planet.

I added, "There is a lot of suffering."

"Enjoy it while you can." He said and then, he disappeared.

I found him less intimidating today, perhaps he realized that he had almost ended my development, by coming through so intensely, the day before.

I thanked him, as well as my Grandpa.

I asked my Grandpa to materialise in my vision. It took a while before he came, but eventually, he stood in front of me and silently lit his pipe. I asked for my Grandma to come through too. At first, I could only hear her say, "I'm here." Then, she showed her face, before fully materialising, linking arms with my Grandpa.

I feel incredibly lucky to have this gift, to be so close to my loved ones in the spirit world. It is so sad that so many people do not have any of these wonderful experiences. In fact, many dismiss it, making fun of it and I have to be very careful who I talk to about such things. This sadly, includes some close relatives.

For those who cannot see their loved ones yet, always remember that they are only a thought away, helping and guiding you, when you need their assistance, all you need to do is ask.

It was not long after, when I visited Little Cote House Hotel with my eldest sister, Meryl. It is reputed to have thirty-two ghosts and the old house dates back to the 1500's. king Henry V111 was said to have met Jane Seymour there. I'm always intrigued about whether I will "see" anything.

I wasn't disappointed, in fact, I had three spirit encounters. The first was during an evening when Meryl and I were in the entertainment hall. There were a lot of people already seated ready for the evening's entertainment to begin, the lights had not yet been dimmed, when I saw the spirit of a black Labrador appear at the side of the stage and run behind the seats. We heard later that the spirit of a similar dog has been seen many times, but usually on a stairway in the old house.

On a couple of occasions, I could smell horses when we took a short cut from our room to the reception, through a covered walkway. This area had harnesses, a plough and an old wooden cart on show, but there were no actual horses. My sister couldn't smell horses at all, but I was overpowered by the smell. I felt the tackle must have held the energies of those horses that used them and I was sensing this.

The third event took place in the library. There was only Meryl and myself in there at the time, I was sitting down and, in my vision, I could see two boys who came and stood in front of me. The older boy of about twelve years old, was wearing an Elizabethan ruff around his neck, usually worn by the rich. The other boy was a bit shorter, probably around ten years old and poorly dressed, I felt he was the gardener's son. The eldest boy told me his name was Henry and the other boy was called Jacob and added that they liked to play in that room. I never did find out who these boys were.

After our stay at Little Cote, we visited our cousin Janet in South Wales, she knows that I do mediumship and wanted me to link into one of the old tea trays that used to belong to our Grandma Tansley, who had been in the spirit world for many years.

I put one of the wooden trays on my knee, its base was decorated with dried flowers, covered with glass and would have been very pretty in its day, but the flowers had faded over the years leaving them quite brown. As I felt the tray and linked in, I could sense that I was standing outside Grandma's haberdashery shop. The front of the shop had a window on either side of the door and all the wood was painted in a dark green colour. Janet, who is four years older than me, had visited the shop on many occasions and was able to confirm this. I don't actually remember going there myself, it was in Birmingham, a long way from Yorkshire and Grandma sadly died when I was only two and a half years old. My Grandpa remarried later after her passing and moved into a house.

In my vision I opened the door and saw an umbrella stand on the floor, it had an intricate decorative leaf pattern cut out of the cast iron from which it was made. There was a walkway to the other side of the room and I was aware of a dark wooden counter on the right-hand side of the shop, on top of which was an old-fashioned till. Janet unfortunately started to give more details about the other side of the room and I had to tell her to stop feeding the medium!

In my vision I walked to the end of the room and took a step down into a narrow corridor, the walls were painted in a dull mustard colour and there were two doors fairly close together. I could see behind one door, a sparsely furnished room with just a table and benches and coat pegs on the wall and felt this was the staff room for the servants and sales girls working for my Grandma.

To my right was a flight of stairs, I walked up them and a short distance along the landing was a door into the lounge. I wasn't shown any furniture, but could see two large sash windows on the other side of the room overlooking the main road. On the right-hand side of the room was a fireplace above which was hanging an oval mirror, I was shown a succession of pictures which had also hung there over the years.

Suddenly, I found myself in the kitchen, there was a butler sink and wooden drainage board positioned under the window. Beside the sink was a large white object that I thought might have been a cupboard, but in fact, Janet told me later that her mother had said it was a fridge. Next to the door was a small table with a heavy brown cloth over it and two chairs pushed under it.

Next, I found myself in Grandma's bedroom, Janet was never allowed in there, so could not confirm the dark wooden dressing table that I saw, with a large mirror which had smaller mirrors on either side set at an angle to it. Grandma was sitting there in front of the mirror combing her hair with an old-fashioned heart-shaped brush on a long handle. My cousin shuddered, she is a bit frightened of spirits, but could confirm most of the rest of what I had described. Some of it she couldn't remember, after all it had been more than sixty years since she had been in the building.

The next day, my Grandpa Tansley came around me, he waited until I had linked in to the spirit world before I could feel his presence. As usual, I found myself in my canoe, Ramonov was sitting at the other end, facing me and I could see his magnificent headdress of long black-tipped white feathers, bound by red twine to the brow band. Today, his face kept changing. First, it was a white man's face, then it changed to the face of a black man. Lots of different faces presented themselves. It made me wonder if he was showing me all the reincarnations of his soul that he had had over time. I still didn't know what his own features looked like.

I said, "Hello, do you want to talk to me?"

"No."

I went on to tell him that I was apprehensive about the change of guide, but I was looking forward to working with him and hoped he would help me with my mediumship.

He said, "I will."

The frightful pain returned to my knee. I asked him to take it away, which he did. Again, it made me wonder if he was putting this pain on me, to signify his presence, or was I still so tense, I was bringing it on myself? As time went by, my meetings with Ramonov did not incur any more pain, I concluded that I had brought it on myself, but marvelled about how he could take the pain away, in the blink of an eye.

I have great faith in spirits' ability to give healing to mortals, here on the earth plane. I am a qualified spiritual healer and channel healing to relatives, friends plus their pets and attend a Healing Centre, as well as being involved in Gentle Approach, a cancer charity. That subject, however will have to wait until I write another book.

My meditation that day, didn't end there. I found myself standing on a street that had a long row of terraced house. It was night time and a girl of about eleven years old, with long dark hair was running down it and went round the corner. Her pace quickened and I followed her, floating behind her. I had never experienced this phenomenon before, I was excited to be able to speed up, to keep pace with her. She passed several people on the way, before disappearing into a doorway.

This event was giving me insight into being able to follow someone or something in my visions and I have had this "flying experience" on several occasions since. On one occasion, I was following a motorcyclist during a message for someone, he was travelling at great speed

along a motorway. I saw a high sided lorry looming up
in the misty distance, he evidently didn't see it and
crashed violently into the back of it, causing him to
summersault backwards and hit his head on the tar-
mac, dying instantly from his head injuries, in spite of
wearing a crash helmet. The recipient of the message
acknowledged a fatal motor cyclist accident, I didn't
give her all the graphic details of course, as I was mind-
ful that the rest of the congregation was listening.

A few days later, I went into meditation again and
had problems trying to visualise my armour on myself.
I had had the same trouble over the last few days and
tried to visualise myself in the Indian canoe, but each
time I did, the canoe became enveloped in a mist
and vanished. I asked Ramonov if I should put on my
armour for protection.

He said, "No."

"Why not?"

He replied, "It is useless."

I asked him, "How should I protect myself then?"

He answered, "I will protect you." I thanked him.

Many mediums have different ideas about protecting themselves when interacting with the spirit world.
Some say that you don't need to protect yourself, others suggest putting an imaginary veil of protection
around yourself, one medium I know, imagines having
fairy dust sprinkled over herself. I go with whatever
my guides suggest.

I have found that Ramonov doesn't visit as often
as my three Indian guides used to do, he only appears
when he has something really important to tell me.

Sometimes, I go into meditation and find myself in complete darkness, I can't hear or see anything. Initially, my Grandpa would come around me, to reassure me that everything was OK, I have spent the time relaxing, clearing my mind of every day matters and enjoying this time completely alone. I come out of these meditations feeling relaxed and refreshed, ready to face the world again.

When Ramonov doesn't appear, I sometimes see other events going on instead. On one occasion, I saw an Indian in a canoe, going horizontally down a waterfall. At the bottom, he started to spear the fish in the water. He collected quite a few and laid them in a neat overlapping row, at the bottom of the boat.

I feel I am given visions like this as a symbol of something. In this instance, I concluded that my spiritual journey may be a bit fraught at times, but there will be rewards at the end.

Later, as my mediumship developed, I was often given signs and symbols tied into the message that I was giving to a person. For example, if I am shown a school bell it is time to be getting on with something that they have been putting off. A Ferris wheel often depicts a person's life going round and round in circles, not knowing which direction to take.

If I see a birthday cake with a slice missing, I know that there has been a birthday recently. If the cake is still whole, then the birthday is still to come in the next few days.

I felt the spirits were teaching me about signs and symbols in my meditations. Sometimes, I had to ask

them what it meant, unfortunately, I didn't always get
an answer, but often when I thought about it, I realised what they were trying to convey. I always find
it intriguing and quite clever, for instance, if I see a
broken bridge, it means there has been a break in a
relationship, a separation. (The bridge linking the two
people together has been broken). A ring placed on
the palm of a hand instead of being put on the wedding ring finger signifies a divorce. Other mediums
may experience different signs and symbols for these
meanings, we are not all the same.

Recently, whilst giving a spiritual message.
I was shown a man in spirit sitting in a wheelchair,
I described him and gave his name. The recipient knew
him immediately. The spirit person proceeded to show
himself in a shirt without a collar and then a shirt with
a collar, indicating that he kept up with the fashion
trends at that time. Apparently, this was quite true of
the man.

The spirits give us these signs and symbols, as it is
much easier than explaining it fully in words. It takes
a great deal of energy for them to come through and
providing the information in this way takes much less
energy.

Now that Ramonov was my guide, I missed the
regular contact that I had with the three Indians and
felt a little abandoned. I went into meditation with
these thoughts, and whilst sitting in my canoe, a man
appeared at the other end. He was dressed in a big fur
coat, light in colour, wearing a hat of similar fur, a long

animal tail attached to the hat hung down his back. His face was quite weather beaten and his mouth was hidden behind a full white bushy beard.

He told me jokingly that he was Father Christmas. I laughed, it was long after Christmas, the end of January in fact and apart from his beard he didn't look at all like Santa and I told him so. He was very friendly, introducing himself as "Helmut." I asked him why he had come. He said, "I like you and want to help." I went on to ask him about a few personal things in my life, he gave me reassurance and the information he gave later became true.

After this, I was left in complete blackness, before the words, "trust in spirit," in large luminous white letters came into view in the distance, the words floated towards me and disappeared off to my right, it was repeated several times.

Another visitor who I had never met when she was on the earth plane was my great grandmother, she has visited me twice now. The first time she came, she sat in a rowing boat with me, wearing black clothes of the Dickensian period. Her long sleeved black dress reached down to her feet and I could see that she was wearing black boots. On her head was a bonnet tied under her chin with black ribbon. She was sitting bolt upright. I didn't know who she was so, I asked her. She replied, "Your great grandmother." Her clothes looked quite expensive and I took her to be my great grandmother on my mother's side as the family had been quite well off, for her husband had been a master shoemaker. Her message was short and sweet, "Best wishes." Probably referring to my spiritual development.

She came another time whilst I was sitting in my Indian canoe during meditation, on this occasion, I could see her black boots in more detail, they were peeping out from her long black dress and I could hear them creaking as she moved. Her boots were fastened with small black shiny buttons which formed a line up the outside of each boot.

She reached into her black beaded handbag perched on her lap and took out a small bottle and handed it to me. I asked permission to take off the cap and fully expected to smell the sweet scent of a fragrant perfume, instead a pungent smell hit my nostrils. I didn't like to say it smelt awful, she read my mind because she said, "Smelling salts". I asked her why she had given them to me, "To revive you," of course that was the Victorians answer to a lot of ailments and I was quite touched that she wanted to help me. I thanked her and she disappeared. Her visit had been quite significant, I had had several infections over those last few months and felt quite low, I needed a bit of reviving.

Once, I experienced mischievous spirits coming through. That night I was just about to fall off to sleep, when I heard the loud bark of a dog right next to my ear, I was startled by the sudden noise and sat bolt upright. In my vision, I could see two teenage spirit boys laughing their heads off, they had done it on purpose to make me jump. I told them to go away and leave me alone. They disappeared and have never been back.

People's souls don't change when they go to the spirit world. If they were pranksters on the earth plane, they will still be pranksters in the spirit world, my Grandpa is a good example! A friend of mine has a spirit guide who is quite a comedian, he must have been a character too, when he was alive on the earth plane.

Ramanov is more serious and was perhaps drawn to my serious energies when he chose to be my guide.

I continued to meditate as often as I could, usually daily at this time in my development and saw different spirit people and experienced many different things. I was giving private readings to friends and my acquaintances and was still attending Development Classes and Open Circles.

That January, I had started to attend a class in Blackburn, after only two weeks, I had been invited by Carol, the Class leader, to be part of a fledgling service. (A spiritual church service in which people who have never been on the platform, have an opportunity to give spiritual messages to people in the congregation.) Carol is a lovely lady and very well-liked, she has been a medium for many years and was always very caring to us all. Our classes were very relaxed and we progressed at our own pace, I felt very comfortable with her. However, during meditation a few days later, my Grandpa told me that I wasn't quite ready for platform mediumship and I didn't feel confident anyway, so I declined. Carol didn't push me, but said to let her know when I was ready.

A few months later, Carol was on holiday and had invited another medium to take our class. Before the class began Sally asked me if I had done any platform work. I told her that I was undecided about this path. She said I was holding myself back. Apparently, Sally had picked up on my energies and could tell that I was clairvoyant, (able to see spirit), clairaudient, (able to hear spirit), clairsentient, (able to sense spirit). She was quite adamant that I would eventually do platform work.

Sometime after that, an Indian appeared during my meditation. I could only see him from his shoulders upwards. He was wearing a magnificent headdress, had brown skin with deep set wrinkles and sunken cheeks. I asked who it was. "Ramonov," came the reply in a deep familiar voice.

I was ecstatic to see him, to view his features properly at last, I had never seen his actual face before, I had seen the rest of him, but never his face until now. It had been six months since he had started visiting me. He said in his commanding voice, "Come, my child be brave and you will go far." I was delighted that he came to give me encouragement and so decided to do the next fledgling service in July, with three other fledglings.

The spirit world must have been pleased because during my next meditation, my oar flew out of my hand and somersaulted three times into the air, before returning. I was then presented with an enormous silver trophy.

It was a few days later when I was in my canoe again, I became quite puzzled, having been given an oar with only one paddle on one end. I thought to myself that I would just be going around in circles if I used it and this is exactly what happened. The water spun around with me making a hole in the centre, like water going down a plughole, as I have experienced before. My canoe whirled down through the hole and entered a tunnel, somehow, I managed to make my way to the end of it, where I was met with a very bright white light. No matter how hard I tried to get closer to this intense light, the canoe didn't move. I felt that they were preparing me for what was to come.

A strange thing happened on the morning of the service. I had been to the supermarket and was unpacking the shopping, when I came to the last item in the last carrier bag, I found a packet of chocolate biscuits. Nothing unusual in that, you might think, but it had not been on my shopping list and wasn't the type of chocolate bar that I normally bought, plus I never bought four at once, being conscious of my figure!

I looked at my shopping receipt and strangely enough the chocolate bars weren't on it. I got out the previous week's shopping receipt, thinking that I had put it in my shopping trolley then by mistake and had not unpacked it. It wasn't listed on there either.

I concluded that it was a present from spirit, a biscuit for each fledgling. I told the other ladies about this strange event after the service and handed them out. We thoroughly enjoyed them and thanked spirit.

Before the service, I had a very memorable meditation, I found myself in my canoe going down a river. At a short distance in front of me stood quite a tall Angel wearing a very luminous tunic, its beautiful wings were outspread and glowed brightly and its golden hair hung in long curls, it stood there holding its hands together as if in prayer. As I approached, it stepped aside to let me pass. (I have referred to the Angel as "it" because they do not have a gender and they have never lived on the Earth plane as a human being).

Not far behind the Angel were huge golden gates which opened to reveal terrific bright white light just like I had seen before. My canoe drifted forward this time and I became engulfed in it, seemingly fusing with it until I was just light itself. An amazing experience.

The service went well and afterwards, one of the ladies to whom I had given a message, said it had been, "spot on". A relative had come through who I identified, wearing a blue dress on which was fastened a brooch, an outfit that was very significant. I was able to describe the spirit lady's personality and give many other details, which is known as evidence, as well as a significant personal message to her. She was ever so grateful and admitted it had brought a tear to her eyes, to know that she had visited.

The booking secretary of another church, attending the service, approached me and asked me if I would do a platform service with an experienced medium, a few days later. There was no hesitation, I accepted straight away! That was the beginning of my platform mediumship.

The next day, whilst meditating, my mother joined me in my canoe, dressed in a 1950's coat and hat, and said she was very proud of me. Next, I found myself on land with Grandpa, he gave me a hug.

He asked me, "What are you going to do now?"

I replied, "Continue."

He clapped his hands, as he knew that I had said to the spirit world, if I did badly, I would never do platform work again.

Then, I found myself in a room in the middle of which stood a three-tier cake resting on a table. There were lots of brightly lit candles arranged on top of the cake and I watched myself blowing them out. I was aware of many spirit people around in the room, but couldn't make out any details, they were only shadows. I blew out the last candle and could see dozens of hands clapping. They were clearly pleased about my decision to continue to do platform work.

When I looked at my numerology forecast for July, which Maria, a friend had done for me, it had come true. The forecast said: "Change is all around you this month. There are opportunities for advancement in a career situation, (I suppose my mediumship can be regarded as a career). Someone important will recognise your talents and the prospects look limitless. Be careful not to rush or be too aggressive. Learn to take your time!

I was awarded the next day during meditation with a golden statue of a man who began to swig back a bottle of beer! It made me laugh. My mother appeared and told me," You have done well and will do well again, keep your chin up." That had been a favourite expression of hers to say, "Keep your chin up," when I was growing up.

However, sometime later, I was still unsure whether to continue doing platform work. My lack of confidence had come back to haunt me once again.

Ramonov appeared in my meditation. "Come my child, walk through the darkness into the light and you will blossom." He led me into a forest and in the middle of it was a clearing and a tall tree was growing in the middle of it, far taller than any of the other trees in the vicinity. I looked up into the sky and saw the sun beaming down. Ramonov pointed to the tall tree and said, "When a tree grows beyond the canopy and sees the sun, it blossoms."

I sensed that he was referring to me. I was so grateful for his faith in me, there is nothing more powerful than those in the spirit world to urge you to go forwards.

The next day, my friend's Joan and Cecily, sisters living in Southport at that time, phoned to tell me that their cat called Kitty was still missing after four weeks. They had been taking her to the cattery a few miles away from their home when they had lost her, she had escaped from her carrier during the walk from the car to the entrance of the cattery, they had spent several hours searching for her, but she was nowhere to be seen.

After the phone call, I went into meditation and asked for kitty to return home. I saw her cleaning herself beside a railway track and when I opened my eyes and turned on the television, the first thing I saw was a train hurtling down a railway track, I felt these events were quite significant. I phoned Joan to tell her what I'd seen and felt that Kitty was near a railway track. She said it was quite possible as the cattery was very close to one.

The next day, I was still concerned. Poor Joan and Cecily were distraught, they had walked for miles each day delivering leaflets with a picture of kitty and their contact details. They weren't sleeping very well from worry. Several people had rung but the cat they had seen, often had a small patch of white fur and Kitty was quite distinctive in that she was very small and totally black.

I was desperate to help in some way and asked spirit to give me guidance. The word "crystal" came into my head. I had done crystal dowsing in an Awareness Class. However, I didn't possess one at the time, though I knew that other items were just as effective. I rummaged through my jewellery box and found a chain with a small metal ball attached, covered in diamante crystals.

I held it up and asked spirit to charge it with energy. when I asked it to swing for a "yes" answer, it swung in a clockwise direction, for a "no" answer, it swung obliquely backwards and forwards. I asked the question, "Is kitty still alive?" Dreading the answer in case it was "no", as it had been four weeks since her disappearance. Thankfully, the ball swung in a clockwise direction, I repeated it a few times to make sure and each time it gave an affirmative answer.

I went to my car to retrieve my A-Z of Southport, this book contained detailed road maps of the area. When I opened it over my dining room table, it dropped out of my hands and flopped open at a certain page, I felt this was very significant too. Sitting down, I held the pendant over the page, asking it to stop at the location of kitty. Suddenly, I felt tremendous energy come into my hand and my hand was moved down the page and towards the right, it stopped over some buildings marked, "works," and significantly, there was a railway alongside it.

I found the power incredible and decided to try it again just to make sure it was correct, I closed my eyes this time and held the pendant out at a distance, the power came back into my hand again and I felt a force moving the suspended ball, sometimes changing direction until it came to a standstill. When I opened my eyes, the ball was directly over the cross I had written previously on the outline of the buildings.

I felt I had to tell Joan and Cecily, but their phone was engaged, so I jumped into the car and drove the seventeen or so miles to Southport. On reaching their house, Joan was out, but Cecily was on the phone taking details about a sighting of kitty. We drove round to that area and on the way, I recounted my experience with the pendant. We met the lady who thought she had seen Kitty, apparently, she had left some tuna fish out for her and when she had called her name, the cat had looked up. We looked around the area of this recent sighting, calling kitty's name and asking people if they had seen her, without any luck.

We decided to go to the area which I had found on my map. Cecily was familiar with that part of town and said it was quite likely that Kitty could be there as the railway passed by both the cattery and the building on my map, which she knew to be a warehouse.

We parked the car and as soon as I got out of it, I could feel the presence of my Grandpa, tightening my throat, it became very intense as we walked alongside the warehouses. We saw a man locking up for the night and showed him a picture of kitty, asking him if he had seen her. Unfortunately, he hadn't seen her, but did told us that they did put food down for cats to encourage them to stay and hopefully kill any mice on the property. As we walked away around the houses the intensity of the tightness in my throat lessened until it disappeared on getting back into the car. My Grandpa had gone.

Apparently, Joan and Cecily had been focusing their search between home and the cattery and this area was beyond the cattery, even further from home.

The next morning, spurred on with my findings, they attached posters to lampposts and posted leaflets into letter boxes of the local houses. When almost finished, they saw a man in his front garden and enquired if he had seen Kitty. He hadn't, but his two girls had said that they had seen a small black cat in the area and thought it was a stray. They had tried to catch it, but it had run away. This gave my friends more encouragement, it was quite likely it was their cat as Kitty hated being picked up by strangers.

Whilst the search was still going on, my spirit father appeared one day, I wasn't even meditating, although I was sitting down thinking about kitty. Only his face manifested itself at the side of me, he told me, "They will find her," and disappeared.

Calls began to come in of sightings, but no one could catch her. Finally, a lady rang to report a cat coming into her garden each evening, similar to the description on the poster and she had been feeding her. Joan and Cecily decided to catch her with a humane cat trap and with the lady's permission, set it down in her garden that evening, containing some appetising food to lure Kitty inside.

Kitty took the bait and was found trapped in the box the next day, looking very much thinner and scruffier than when my friends had last seen her. Nevertheless, they were delighted to be reunited with her once more. I thanked spirit for their help. I was happy to have assisted in some way and to initially have given my friends hope that Kitty was still alive.

I continued to meditate most days, sometimes, things would appear on the seat at the other end of the canoe. One day, a teddy bear appeared wearing a Scottish tam-o-shatter on his head, it was quite significant as I had just finished reading a murder mystery set in the Shetland Isles. That day, I was paddling the canoe just off the coast and navigating myself through dozens of chalk arches in the cliffs.

I asked, "Why are all these arches here?"

I could hear Ramonov's voice say, "This is how far you have come."

I took this to mean, how far I had come in my spiritual development, so I said, "I bet I still have a long way to go."

Immediately, I saw dozens more arches, all the way up to the sky, quite a long way to go still. In fact, you never stop learning mediumship until the day you pass over.

On other occasions, my meditations give insights into future events. I remember one time when my oar turned into an arrow which shot off into the sky and burst a balloon and notes of money showered over me. A few days later a cheque for £60, arrived through the post, a refund from a catalogue, that I had forgotten about.

Spirits are always trying to let you know that they are around and are there when certain things happen. One day, my paddle changed into the full skeleton of a fish, the paddles at each end of the oar, became the head and the tail. This was quite significant too, as the day before I had been eating mackerel and although it should have been filleted, I found an entire length of bone in it. A spirit person must have been around me and witnessed it.

Once when I meditated following a service that I had done. I found myself in the canoe once more, this time as an Indian boy of about seven or eight years old. I had been given a very large paddle, much larger than normal. Ramanov was sitting at the other end of the canoe, with a bright light shining above. I asked him why I had been given such a big paddle, "Because you have done well," came the kind reply.

I gave the oar back to him, telling him I felt that he deserved it more than me. Old problems in the family had risen up again and I couldn't bring myself to forgive the family member involved, consequently, I didn't feel worthy of receiving the huge oar. (Thankfully, I have been able to forgive the person since. Holding onto negative feelings doesn't do anyone any good at all).

The next day, whilst meditating, the large oar just dropped on my lap, Ramanov was nowhere to be seen. I was delighted, he evidently still felt that I deserved it.

The oar did many other things as well, I remember seeing it once, rising out of my hand into the air to become the arrow on a weather vane. At the time I wasn't sure why this had happened, but it wasn't long before it became clear.

I was staying with my sister at the time and we had decided that evening to watch the DVD; "Nights of

Rodanthe". To my surprise the same weather vane that I had seen in my meditation was featured in it.

Ramanov was not only kind and reassuring, but gave healing to my granddaughter, who was still alive on the earth plane. He came gently holding her one day, and I could feel his love for her. She was born with problems in her hips and had to spend many months in a plaster cast. I asked Ramanov if he would heal her, he said he would do his best, then, he turned to me and said, "Bless you." Then he looked at my granddaughter and gave her his blessing too.

His healing that day worked wonders as my grand-daughter was able to have the cast removed at eight months old and could walk by the time that she was twelve months old! She went on to attend gymnastic classes and could walk a couple of miles by the time she was two. I am so grateful to Ramanov and very proud of my granddaughter.

Ramanov came to give me reassurance on many occasions, one time, I was a bit concerned about my finances, as my tenant had moved out of my other house and the house was still empty. I was left having to pay council tax and standing charges, above all my other expenses, making money a bit tight.

Naturally, Ramanov was aware of this and during meditation he appeared sitting at the other end of my canoe, between us was a large fridge-freezer with a bowl of fresh fruit on the top. The doors opened to show that it was jam-packed with a variety of food.

Ramanov spoke, "You will always have plenty," then disappeared.

Sure enough, I have never been without and it wasn't long before a new tenant took up residence. The meditation that day didn't end there however, ahead of me, I could see a headland looming. On it was scaffolding supporting a billboard with huge fluorescent white letters spelling, "Happy Birthday." Fireworks began to go off all around it, making a spectacular multicoloured scene of flashes and sparkles. A marvellous spectacle.

It was of course very significant, my birthday was in 9 days.

He reassured me again a few months later, when my paddle became a rocket and flew into the sky. On the ground, I saw Indian's dancing in a circle. Ramanov held a starting pistol, very similar to the one my Dad had had. He fired it, saying, "This is the start, you will do well." At this point I had decided to start writing this book, Ramanov added, "The book will be published."

Writing this book had given me something to do during the Christmas fortnight when the spiritual churches had closed and all my clubs and groups had shut for the holidays. Unfortunately, once the holidays were over, I didn't have time to finish it and it wasn't until the lockdowns during the coronavirus pandemic that I sat down and completed it two years later.

Not long after, I was booked to give a service and a few days beforehand I was given a long oar during meditation, a sign that I was doing well. It broke into two pieces as I entered a dark tunnel, which was quite low and turned from left to right. As I came around the corner, there was a bright white light ahead, wrought iron gates opened and I could see a magnificent luminescent Angel with wings spreading wide, reaching each side of the tunnel. I drew closer, the Angel turned sideways to allow me through and I went into the light and as I did so, I seemed to fuse with it, my body and the light were one and the same. The energies began to change around me and I felt healing.

The service went well, several people who had received messages came up to me afterwards to thank me.

The next day, I was awarded with a long paddle, spirit must have thought that I had done well, but quite unexpectedly, the oar shortened before my eyes to become a dart. A dart board appeared and the dart was thrown into the bull's eye, a symbol to convey I was spot on with my messages at the service.

A young man appeared opposite me with black curly hair wearing a black cloak. He dropped his cloak from his shoulders and handed me a square-shaped box. I took the lid off and inside was a heart shaped wooden box with a hinged lid. Inside that was a tiny toy soldier, I felt it symbolised my soldiering on with my mediumship. The soldier disappeared and it was several seconds before my father materialised out of the heart and said, "Well done," and walked off.

Next Grandpa emerged from the heart he started to clap his hands declaring, "You did it!" My Grandma followed saying, "You are very special Viv."

I asked for my mother, I could sense an energy around me and I heard her say, "I am around you all the time, I don't need to come."

Next, I found myself at a party, I could hear party poppers being pulled. Someone was putting a slice of Victoria sponge cake, coated with icing and small coloured decorations, into my mouth, I couldn't actually taste it though. I raised my wine glass and said, "Cheers." Many voices repeated cheers too, although I couldn't see them, I felt quite emotional that they were having a party for me to celebrate having done another service.

Not long after this, I gave a service at Cleveley's Spiritual Church and was asked if I would do some more.

The next day, during meditation my oar got longer and longer, before rising out of my hands and snapping in two, turning into two brooms. I had to smile, spirit must have been around me when I was busy sweeping up that morning.

Sometimes, Ramanov visited to try and cheer me up if I was a bit down in the dumps. In one particular meditation, I saw a cowboy playing a guitar and there was Ramanov clapping in time to the music, saying that he was bringing me joy. It always gives me upliftment to think that the spirit world picks up on my moods and try to help.

Ramonov was always ready to help me, often with a sense of humour. One day he was sitting in my canoe and a pair of gloves suddenly appeared on my hands, they were far too big for me, in fact they were several sizes too big. Puzzled, I queried, "What's the significance of these?"

He didn't answer, just gave a wry smile and lit his long clay pipe, I could smell the smoke, which began to curl up and dissipate into the air.

Thinking about the oversized gloves later that the day, I came to the conclusion that they were to give me a helping hand. On a previous occasion, if you remember I had asked for a helping hand and the top of my oar turned into a blown-up plastic glove!

The next time that I saw Ramanov, he commented, "So you managed to work it out."

Then a heavy object manifested itself on my lap. It was a very large ladle about a metre in length. I had no idea what it meant and had to ask him. "Ladle it out to them," he urged. I took this to mean my mediumship. I was in fact going to an Open Circle that evening, which was very successful.

A few days later, before Christmas, Grandpa was tightening my throat, a sign that I needed to go into meditation. I found myself sitting in my canoe and Santa Claus stood up, took my paddle and put a small ornamental Christmas tree with lights on, into my hand. He walked off, leaving me without my paddle and I wondered how I was going to go forwards without it. I could hear Ramonov's voice say, "The tree will grow to dizzy heights and will provide you with a paddle."

I said, "That will take a long time."

"Have patience," he replied.

I didn't have to wait long before twenty oars or more, fell across my canoe. "Now you have enough oars to go forward." I heard him say. I remembered that there is no time in the spirit world and trees can grow in no time, if that is what is wished for. I also felt that these oars had been given symbolically to indicate that I have everything I need now to move forward with my mediumship.

He has often come to me in meditation holding a baby, when someone in the family has just become pregnant and the word is not yet out. However, I'm not always given a clue about the baby's sex, as on this particular occasion, when he presented me with a baby wrapped in a white blanket. Curious, I naturally asked who it was and Ramanov told me it was a baby yet to be born. Eight months later one of my nieces delivered a healthy baby boy.

A medium once told me that there would be a September baby born into the family and sure enough, my daughter who wasn't even pregnant at the time, gave birth to a little baby boy early in September.

It was not just Ramanov who visited me in my canoe, one day a lady whom I had never seen before, sat at the other end of the canoe. She wore a fur coat and matching hat and said her name was Nina, she said she was bestowing self-pride on me.

It was appropriate, I was feeling a little low, as I had proofread a friend's book and asked if I could go through it once again. Proofreading wasn't something I had done before and I wanted to make sure everything was correct. Unfortunately, she was in a hurry to self-publish and went ahead. I purchased the book and of course there were a few errors, which didn't make me feel good about myself at all.

Having explained this to the spirit stranger, she smiled, "You do well and will do well." I thanked her.

My Grandpa came around me, tightening my throat and although I couldn't see him, he gently reassured me saying that seeds grow into big apples and a large apple came into my vision. I'm for ever grateful for his reassurance and faith in me. Ramanov would give me words of wisdom too.

Over the last day or so, I had been dwelling on incidents of bullying during my childhood. Silly I know, doing that after so many years, but those terrible times sometimes rear up without warning and bring back the stress and depression.

Ramanov appeared next to me on the bench, during a talk-through meditation at a Development Class. He gave me valuable advice that day saying, "The tempest is over, move forward and strike out again!"

For anyone reading this who has suffered from any kind of abuse, they are wise words. We cannot do anything about the past and dwelling on it does no-one any good, the best action is to move forward and try not to look back, move on with your life.

Ramanov has also come to tell me about future events. I remember being in a cave in my canoe one time, as I went into meditation. I glided out into a still lagoon and on the horizon, I could see land from which a very big plume of grey smoke rose high into the sky. At the top of this plume was black smoke, fanning out horizontally.

Ramanov had joined me in the canoe and I asked him what it was. He replied, "There is going to be a big fire." He was right of course, five days later the huge McIntosh building named the Glasgow School of Art, sadly went up in flames and was very badly damaged.

On his next visit Ramanov, drew a semi-circle in the air with his index finger, explaining that was how far I had come with my mediumship and told me, I would complete the circle.

He also warned me about another future event and told me not to go to a group hypnosis session in which we were going to go into past life regression. It was early in the evening, approaching 5.30 pm and I was sitting in my lounge, I could see many spirit energies flitting about, not unusual except that they didn't come around me this early. I felt Grandpa's familiar tightening of my throat, so I went into meditation. I became aware of Ramanov sat at a table talking to my Dad. I asked why they were there together. Ramanov replied, "Because you are his child." I felt their meeting was about me going to the Past Life Regression Session.

I asked, "Shouldn't people do this?"

"No, you will be affected by what you see."

"Will it help me in my life today?" I asked.

"No"

I was really disappointed that Ramanov didn't want me to go, because I had been looking forward to it very much. All that evening I was torn between listening to him and going to experience the past life regression.

Finally, I made up my mind. I was going to go. I couldn't imagine that anything could upset me, after all I had been a nurse for forty-one years and had seen some dreadful things. What's more, I had already paid for the session. My mind was made up!

The next day, I drove to Chorley where it was to take place. On the way Grandpa was tightening my throat, letting me know he was there.

We sat in a circle and introduced ourselves, Kathy, who was in charge give us an explanation of the proceedings. She had brought along a helper in case one of us needed extra guidance.

We first experienced a lighter regression. Kathy talked to us in a gentle tone, asking us to relax, before we descended an imaginary flight of steps and sat on a couch in the room below. There she asked us to relax further and talked about a door to our right-hand side on which was a red and green button.

The green button when pressed would open the door, but the red button could be pressed if we wanted to come back to the couch. At any time during the regression, we could imagine the red button and press it to return.

In this relaxed state, Kathy asked us to walk to the door, visible in our trance. At this point she said, if you have changed your mind and don't want to proceed you can press the red button and go back to the couch.

I took the bold decision to press the green button, even though Ramonov's words hung over me.

I opened the imaginary door and found myself in a wonderful Japanese garden, beautiful pink blossom hung from trees, with twisty trunks and branches. It was a lovely day; the sky was a perfect blue and the sun was shining brightly. I walked up a straight path aware that I was wearing a brightly coloured yellow kimono, patterned with large flowers. My hair was jet black, tied back into a bun on the back of my head and I was wearing a kind of sandal made of wood.

Ahead of me was a Japanese house supporting a long sloping roof that curled up at the corners. Inside was a room with a low table, I found myself kneeling at the table and on my left were my children, a girl of five years old and a boy of three years old. Across the table from me was my grandfather with a Mandarin-type of moustache, I knew I respected him, but didn't like him at all.

Suddenly, the walls began to shake and I looked around in terror, huge amounts of black water began to gush in through the window behind me. I could hear the children screaming, then felt a terrible blow on the back of my head and everything went black.

I imagined the red button we had been told about and pressed it. Immediately, I felt as if I was being sucked out of the room and found myself back on the couch.

That was quite an experience.

I must have been a well-off Japanese lady in a past life who was caught up in, possibly a tsunami and thankfully didn't suffer going through an actual drowning, for I was knocked unconscious beforehand.

The other ladies had had different experiences of course. Unfortunately, one lady had not had a past life regression at all and had just seen colours and felt healing energies around her.

We had a short break before we were taken into a deeper regression. Kathy asked us to go to a safe place in our minds, I choose to sit in my Indian canoe. She then slowly read a script, which took us along a hallway where there were many doors, behind each there was a past life. We had to allow our subconscious mind to take us to the right door and open it.

Before we were told to open the door, I had already become a boy of about eight or nine years old pulling a wooden hand cart along a cobbled street. The cart was full of chopped wood and I could feel that my face and hands were dirty and I was dressed in rags.

I found myself elsewhere, standing on a quayside looking at a three-mast ship moored in the harbour. I yearned to be on the ship and as I gazed at it, I could feel the cold cobbles beneath my bare feet.

Suddenly, the scene changed again and I was mopping the decks of the same ship, dogs were sleeping peacefully in the corner. I became an observer at this point and could see an angry man slapping me across my face. I became the boy again, sitting down on the deck with my knees drawn up and I was hugging my knees as tightly as I could, feeling very sorry for myself. An old man came over to me and started talking to me. I couldn't hear exactly what he was saying, but knew that he was being kind to me.

Kathy interrupted, asking us to go forward in time.

I found myself on a canal barge, I was a grown man by now, in my early twenties, steering the boat, aware of grain in the hold.

Kathy asked us to move forward to the final moments of that life.

I was much older, probably in my forties quietly advancing towards an old man whose back was turned to me. He was busy counting his money which he kept in a large tin box. He looked a bit like Fagan from Oliver Twist, as his back was a little bit hunched and his coat was dark and dingy and his scraggly long grey hair fell about his shoulders.

I raised my knife and stabbed him with a great deal of force in his back. In my trance I had no misgivings at all about doing this dreadful act.

Then, I found myself in a room, and saw an official-looking man sitting behind a desk with a document in front of him, he was signing it with a quill. Presumably, this was my death warrant.

Ramanov came to my side and for what seemed an age, I didn't see anything. I was in complete blackness and began to think that my regression had finished.

Then, I saw that a man had been hanged outside in a courtyard. There was a crowd of people still watching and I stood there with them looking at him dangling from the gallows, knowing that that was my body hanging there, I was numb without any feelings of remorse for murdering the old man, my spirit looking at my dead body.

We were brought out of the hypnosis.

No wonder Ramanov had not wanted me to go that day, but in spite of ignoring his advice, he was still there for me protecting me from the worst of it all. He had made me an observer, when I was being slapped around the face by that angry man on the ship and most importantly of all, had put me into blackness during the hanging, to save me the agony of experiencing being throttled to death.

I'm very grateful to Ramanov for his help and glad he was there, he didn't abandon me when I had ignored his advice, but I'm still glad that I went and experienced what I did and I have had no ill effects from my experiences of that day.

I must have learned a lesson from murdering that man in my past life, as in this life, I can't even kill insects in my house, I capture them and let them loose into the garden and apologise to snails, if I accidently tread on them.

My whole life has been given over to caring for people and animals. During my teens as I've mentioned before, I spent most of my spare time working on a dairy farm with my twin sister, milking the cows and looking after the calves. We also cared for the horses and "broke in" the young ponies.

Later, I trained to be a nurse and spent my entire career caring for people and during my retirement, I've qualified as a spiritual healer, channelling healing to many ill people and as you know I'm also a medium, giving messages of love and comfort to people from their spirit relatives.

It is believed by many, that we are born time and time again, to live lives on this earth and learn lessons to improve our soul. Eventually, when we have learned all our lessons, there is no need for us to return anymore, for by that time our souls are pure, enabling us to ascend to a much higher plane.

Ramonov continued to give me confidence. I had had a number of bookings for spiritual churches and was hoping that I didn't let anyone down. Back in my canoe, I found myself in an infinity pool and I suddenly dropped over the edge, becoming a horse with wings which took off into the sky, flying over the deep blue sea below. Beautiful mountains rose up in the distance, lit up by the bright sunshine. I could hear Ramonov say, "You will do well!"

I wasn't quite sure what the significance of the flying horse was until a few days later, when I was given a large oar, signifying that Ramonov was pleased with me, but I was in a very tiny canoe, in fact, it was so tiny that I could barely fit in it, my knees were up to my chest, a sign that I'm not thinking big. I knew what he meant, I asked him, "So, should I do Divine Services on my own?" meaning that I should start to do the philosophy myself, as soon as I said that, the canoe grew bigger to become the usual size.

I had been taking my friend, John to the first couple of services, so that he could give the philosophy and some of the messages. Maria, another friend, had also helped me out at a service. It was a bit of support, but now it was evidently time for me to go it alone. I didn't feel too bad about it, as I had Ramonov's blessing, which gave me a great deal of confidence.

Just then a white luminous horse grew large wings and flew off into the sky. I guessed it was probably Pegasus, but again I didn't know the significance, so I looked it up. Apparently, many people use Pegasus as a symbol, when they want success, Pegasus went on to greatness.

Ramanov came again a few days later, sitting in my seat, whilst I was sitting on the side of the canoe cuddling a Siberian Husky puppy. It wriggled out of my hands and ran to Ramanov to be petted. I thanked him for paddling the canoe and was just about to start reading a book when he interrupted me saying, "Come my child be brave and you will go far." I remember him having said this before when I was reluctant to do my first service as a fledgling.

He continued, "It is for me to direct you my child, I am your guide." Later, he said, "Be calm my child, you will do well."

Surprisingly, a brown bear appeared in my canoe the next day, sitting in my seat. He threw the paddle to me and I threw it back to him. He threw it back again and I tried to paddle with it, but the canoe went nowhere. I gave up and threw it back to him, he began to paddle and the canoe moved steadily in the water, but stopped on the edge of a waterfall. A sign that spirit wants me to take the plunge of going it alone at the divine church services.

On the day of my solo Divine Service, I could feel my Grandpa tightening my throat during my meditation beforehand, he had come to give me reassurance. Ramanov was paddling the canoe, sitting in my seat. We went along the river and descended comfortably down the waterfall. When we finally reached still waters below, Ramanov reached forward to place a ring with a sapphire stone, on my wedding ring finger. Puzzled, I asked, "Why?"

He replied, "You are married to spirit now."

The Divine Service went well and several people said they enjoyed it. In fact, the chair person who is an experienced medium, commented that I was a breath of fresh air, describing the spirit relatives that came through, she claimed that a lot of mediums, don't do that.

In my next meditation, Ramanov came smoking his clay pipe, congratulating me. I asked him, "Where do I go from here?" Anywhere you want to, was his gentle reply.

I found myself in a room, standing behind a table with an enormous five-tier cake which almost reached the ceiling. On the top of it were statues of a bride and groom. I remembered Ramonov having said that I was married to spirit now, this was obviously my wedding cake. I could hear clapping and "Well done." Shrill wolf whistles could be heard above the noise. Unfortunately, I couldn't see anyone, until I went into another room where there was a circle of people sitting on chairs, passing around a very large clay pipe, taking a turn at smoking it, then passing it on to the next person. I didn't recognise anyone except my father, probably the others were his relatives, as I didn't meet many of them, when they were here on the earth plane.

In those early days, I was always given a party after having done a service and was very grateful to spirit for their kindness and encouragement. Each of these parties had a different theme. I will mention some of these later.

Following another service, I was looking down at my canoe from a bank at the side of the river, not knowing why I wasn't sitting in it. Ramanov said it was because I was elsewhere and so I was. I found myself walking up a long flight of stone steps up to a majestic castle. Lots of people were lining the steps, cheering and clapping as I passed, seemingly congratulating me after having done a service the day before.

Inside the castle, I entered a large room and at the end of it sat a man, dressed a bit like Robin Hood sat on a throne of carved wood. Either side of him were similar thrones which were empty. I sat next to him on his left-hand side.

Thinking about the significance of this later, I felt I was being thanked for all the ways that I help people, just as Robin Hood had done in the legend. I feel that giving messages from spirit relatives and friends, helps to comfort people and let them know that their relatives are not dead, but very much alive, just living on a different energy plane. I know that the healing energy that I also channel can help a great deal and go a long way to helping people's ills and mental health.

Spirit relatives are watching over their loved ones, helping them to make their dreams and wishes come true, guiding them down the right path and often giving healing, as well as lots of love. If you ever need help or guidance, they are only a thought away, your thoughts and prayers will be heard. Those in the spirit world will do their best to make things happen, if they can.

Sadly, for me, it was soon to be the last time (or so I thought), that Ramonov would come to see me, as a new guide called Ismos had introduced himself. I have written a chapter about Ismos later. However, after Ismos's initial meeting, he didn't appear and ten days went by with still no sign of him.

I was left confused about who would be my guide at the next service. Ramanov must have read my thoughts as he joined me in the canoe and said, "The transition will be complete by Sunday." I was due to do another service then.

I saw Ramanov for the last time a few days later, when he appeared in my canoe. He said, "Congratulations!" I asked him what the congratulations was for after all,

I hadn't done the service. "For all the services that you will be doing this year,"

It was true, I had been booked for thirteen services at that point in time and it was only early January. I thanked him and I asked if I would do well. "You will do well, my child."

I turned to see three cowboys firing rifles at Ramanov from the bank. I was horrified and quickly got to my feet, shouting at them to stop and go away, which they did, but when I looked back at Ramanov, he had gone.

It made me wonder if that was how he passed over, shot down by a bunch of cowboys. How cruel! I thought I would never see him again and was quite sad, but he wasn't quite gone, his voice broke the silence, "You will go much further."

Admittedly, it had been a wobbly start with Ramanov, when he had half scared me to death during our first encounter. Eventually however, I had truly grown to love him. He had taught me many things and it was through his constant reassurances and congratulations when I had done well at church services, Development Classes, as well as Open Circles, that my confidence grew.

When I doubted myself, he took over the paddling of my canoe, until a time that he saw fit for me to paddle it again.

I feel I owe him a great deal, for he has helped me to go forward along my spiritual path in leaps and bounds, for which I will be eternally grateful. I will miss him very much.

Chapter **8**

Grandpa

I thought I would devote a chapter to my dear Grandpa, who you already know, has helped me a great deal along my spiritual path.

My Grandpa, on my mother's side, was a lovely man, who sadly passed when I was only seven years of age. We lived in Yorkshire back then and he lived quite a distance away in Birmingham, so we didn't see him very often.

Unfortunately, I have only a couple of memories of him, but these memories have stayed with me. The first I recall, was when he was staying at our house in Batley. On that particular day, I had come home from school crying, as I had bumped my head, walking into a lamp-post, (obviously not looking where I was going}. It had given me a thumping headache and I was feeling rather sorry for myself.

When I entered the dining room, my Grandpa was standing there warming himself in front of the coal fire. He asked me why I was crying, so I told him what I had done. He said quite seriously, "Well, why would you do that?" I saw the funny side and began to laugh, my tears soon dried and the unfortunate incident was forgotten.

My Grandpa was a practical joker when he was alive, as I've said before and liked to make people laugh, my mother also told me that he loved children very much. His personality, hasn't changed of course, in the spirit world.

My only other memory of him was during a visit to see him in Birmingham at his house. That particular day my family and I were all travelling in his car, going to visit my Grandma's cremation plaque at the cemetery. En route, the car filled up with smoke and we all had to pile out, onto the pavement. Quite frankly, I was expecting the car to burst into flames at any moment, but my Grandpa tinkered about under the bonnet for a while and soon everything was in order and we journeyed on again. I was impressed, even at that young age, with his calmness and how he made everything into a joke.

In the first chapter, I briefly mentioned how he came around me when I was a bit down, filling the bedroom with the smell of tobacco smoke, bringing me peace and calm. Grandpa has remained with me since then and visits me regularly during my meditations, giving me praise, encouragement, advice and plenty of reassurance.

The first time that I actually saw him, I was about to go to an Awareness Class, this was in the early days of my development. I could smell tobacco smoke in the bedroom, whilst I was putting on my shoes and I could detect the smoke in the hallway before I left the house. During my meditation at the class, he stood before me in my vision and casually lit his pipe, then quite unexpectedly, he clapped his hands and said, "Well Done." Praise, for managing to see him at last.

He came not long after this giving me advice, he was standing in a rowing boat, fishing and said "You have got to learn to catch the tiddlers, before catching the big fish." I was always wanting to be much further ahead in my development at the time and he was basically telling me to learn to take it step by step.

When he visited the Awareness Class again shortly afterwards, Mary our teacher, could smell tobacco smoke as I arrived. I was the first person there and told her that it was probably my Grandpa, although I could not smell the smoke myself, on that occasion. She could see him sitting in a chair at the other side of the room. He was asking me for his name, of course, I just knew him as Grandpa, but did know that his surname was Tansley. "That will do," he told Mary.

Then, he came to sit in the chair next to me. Unfortunately, I still couldn't see him, I only ever saw him during meditation and wished that I could see him sitting next to me, I expressed this to Mary, my Grandpa must have heard, as through her, he told me to work on it.

Mary said that he had come to help me during the class, as it needed a certain amount of trust and she knew and so did he, that I trusted him.

When Linda arrived, a few minutes later, she saw my Grandpa sitting next to me, she linked in with him, described him perfectly and told me that he was a lovely man, naturally I agreed.

The exercise that evening involved inviting our spirit guides to come very close around us, during our meditation and then to ask them to draw back, so that we could feel the difference in the energies around us. We repeated it three times.

I felt a strong vibration each time my guide drew close, other members of the circle felt hot or cold, or had the sensation of pins and needles.

Grandpa has come around me ever since, when I am needing reassurance. At first, I would see glimpses of him during meditation, then he started to give me the sensation of my throat tightening to let me know he was around me. (He had suffered from throat cancer, which spread to his lungs before he passed over, this was probably how his throat had felt). Very rarely do I smell his tobacco smoke now.

Grandpa came to give me reassurance on another occasion, he started tightening my throat when I was meditating in my canoe and a cloaked figure had appeared at the other end. I had no idea who it was and felt a little apprehensive, as I couldn't see the person's face, but I trusted my Grandpa to keep me safe.

We were travelling along on a river, going under bridges and although it was dark, I could make out the shadows of tall buildings and could see lights in the windows.

I asked the person to reveal themselves, the cloak fell away and there, sat in my canoe, was a beautiful young Angel, saying, "Thank you for trusting in spirit."

A few days earlier, I had been given a scroll during meditation, but was unable to read it, the writing wasn't clear, now was the perfect opportunity to ask the Angel what it had said. The Angel replied, "This is just the beginning."

Not long after, my Grandpa came around me in his usual fashion and I asked him how he was, he said, "Splendid." I enquired if I was going to be a medium. He replied, "In time." He was right, it was about a year after this that I did my first service, giving mediumship from the platform.

I was quite over-whelmed, it seemed that my destiny was already mapped out. Just then, I saw a diver jumping off a high spring board into the deep water below. I felt this was a sign that I was making the jump and advancing in my career of mediumship.

Much later in my development, my Grandpa was there again, reassuring me during meditation, before I was to give spiritual communication at a service. I found myself in my canoe as usual going through a tunnel. There were Angels standing on each side at the end of the tunnel and I could see an Angel sat high on a marble seat at the top of a flight of steps. My canoe came to a halt at the bottom of them. The Angel spoke, "You will do well." Presumably, referring to the service and I have to say that I felt it did go well.

Later, during my development, he would tighten my throat as an indication to go into meditation, so that he could tell me something important. Sometimes

I would be washing up or doing housework and would have to tell him to hang on.

One of these occasions turned out to be a warning. When I was eventually in meditation, he showed me a vision of me driving down a country road at night, with a lady passenger. A few yards up the road on the other side, was a white van travelling towards us. Suddenly, a red car came out from behind the white van to overtake it and swerved in front of us, in order to get back into the other lane. We almost had a head-on crash.

I asked my Grandpa, "When is this going to happen?"

"Today!"

That evening, I had planned to take a female friend for a meal and the journey was to take us down a country road. Needless to say, I went a lot slower than I would have normally driven. Halfway down this country lane, I saw a white van approaching, it was similar to the one I had seen in meditation, I slowed even more and as predicted a car suddenly shot out from behind the van to overtake it, not even giving a tentative glance beforehand, to see if the coast was clear. Thankfully, I was going quite slowly, so this driver had a chance to get back into his own lane, before crashing head long into us. He had been driving quite fast and it was dark, so I couldn't see the colour of the vehicle, but I bet it was red!

I heaved a sigh of relief and silently thanked my Grandpa. Now that I can link with him and speak with him, I no longer have those dreadful forebodings that

I experienced earlier in my life. Grandpa can tell me what is going to happen and so I am better prepared.

On another occasion I found myself paddling my canoe in the open sea, surrounded by sharks who were swimming around my canoe, I heard him say "Watch out for danger."

Later that day, I drove into Southport to do some shopping, it was the busiest I had ever seen it and naturally due to the warning I took extra care.

There were no problems on the way there, it wasn't until I had finished my shopping and had returned to my car in the carpark that things started to happen. I began to reverse out of my space, when the man in the car opposite suddenly reversed out without hesitation and without it seems noticing me at all. I quickly drove forward again to prevent a collision.

On the journey home, I drove very carefully heeding the warning, when another driver coming from the opposite direction, almost collided with me after overtaking another vehicle. I had to swerve to avoid a head-on collision and ended up in the gutter.

Much more recently, I intended to go a Divine Service at my local church to which I go every Sunday, it was still open at times during the covid pandemic when the number of cases and deaths were fairly low. However, a few hours before I was due to set off, I felt the now familiar tightening of my throat and began to meditate, I heard him say, "Don't go!" He repeated those words.

Quite honestly, I thought I was imagining it because I really wanted to go, everyone had been in lockdown for a few months and the restrictions had now been relaxed, allowing us to go to services and meet everyone, albeit two metres apart with masks on. As I was thinking this, I was shown a crystal on a chain.

My Grandpa wanted to prove that what he had said was true. I fetched my crystal on a chain, I did the usual preparation of determining which way it was going to swing for a "yes" or a "no" answer. It swung clockwise for "yes" and didn't move at all for "no." Then, I asked the question, "Should I go to the service?" The crystal stood still, even if I moved it, it came to a sudden halt so quickly that it was a physical impossibility. I asked, "So, I haven't to go to the Service?" The crystal moved energetically in a clockwise direction. I waited to see if it would stop and it carried on whizzing round and round for several minutes until my arm was aching so much, I had to stop holding the chain.

I got the message loud and clear as it were and was in no doubt that Grandpa didn't want me to go. He stayed with me tightening my throat until the time came when I would normally have set off in the car, I decided to take his advice though and stayed at home. It must have been very important that I shouldn't go out that night, perhaps he could see an accident or maybe I would have contracted coronavirus at the church. I will never know.

Grandpa can be serious sometimes, but often he shows his other side bringing humour and little pranks though into my meditations.

When I go into meditation, I imagine opening up my seven main chakras, these are energy centres positioned down the centre of the body which have the same colour and order as a rainbow: The first is the root chakra situated at the base of the spine, which vibrates to the same frequency as the colour red, followed by the sacral chakra (orange), then the abdominal chakra (yellow), next the heart chakra (green), up to the throat chakra (blue), followed by the brow chakra (indigo) and lastly, the crown chakra at the top of the head, which has the same frequency as violet. When opening up to the spirit world I imagine these colours as I open each chakra.

Grandpa made me laugh once, when I saw fluffy dusters in the appropriate colours coming out of each chakra. He must have been around that day when I was dusting. Other times, I may see flowers emerging from my chakras.

One day, I was definitely not paying attention and got the order of the colours wrong, Grandpa took all the colours and mixed them all together! It did make me laugh. Later on, in my development I found that I didn't need to think about opening each chakra, just going into the quiet for a second or two is sufficient now, to link with the spirit world.

One summer, I grew sunflowers in the garden and all the time they were growing, Grandpa had a sunflower rising out of the top of my head! (I was standing a few feet away watching myself.) These were no ordinary sunflowers they had smiley faces. Each time I went into meditation and opened my crown chakra, the sunflower would be doing something different;

blowing kisses or blowing bubble gum into a huge bubble. On other occasions, the sunflower would be standing on a ladder, waving at me or would have bright red cherry lips. The antics of these sunflowers are too numerous to mention, but they always made me smile. Finally, when I chopped down the plants at the end of summer, I never saw them again during meditation.

Grandpa continued to amuse me though, one time a dandelion emerged, grew old and went to seed, someone blew the seeds away. On coming out of meditation the first thing I saw was a book that I was reading: "Dandelion Summer," by Lisa Wingate. He was just letting me know that he is often around me and knows what I'm doing.

Another time when opening my chakras, I could see myself coming out of my crown chakra drinking tea out of an old-fashioned white enamelled mug with a blue rim, then found myself on a ladder watering a tree using a teapot! My Grandpa is such a scream and I have to smile, he must have been in my art class that morning, when we had been discussing teapots.

Once I was thinking of buying a bottle of Prosecco, to celebrate my friend's new house purchase, needless to say, Grandpa was one step ahead, for in the morning during meditation, before buying the Prosecco, I found myself halfway up a pole, slugging back a bottle of champagne!

A few days later, I had been washing out old jars in the morning, with the idea of painting and decorating them. Naturally, Grandpa wanted to let me know he had been around me, this time I was clinging to a pole with hooks, upon which were suspended lovely decorated jars.

At Christmas time, he sent Santa riding on a go-kart with a pile of presents, tied with a red ribbon! The next day, Santa was an ice statue sitting on his sleigh – I often wonder, what ever will he dream up next.

Grandpa was also there with me one Christmas Day, when I was alone for part of the day. I was busy watching a programme on the TV, when I could feel the familiar tightening of my throat. I asked him to hang on until the programme had finished, but he continued to persist, making the feeling more and more intense. I gave up trying to watch the telly and went into meditation. I'm glad I did.

I found myself in a rowing boat which was gliding through the water on its own. At the other end of the boat sat a man, serenading me with his guitar, I didn't know who he was, as I couldn't see him clearly, I just sat back and enjoyed the music and the singing. We entered a dark tunnel and I could feel the closeness of the damp walls.

Coming out of the tunnel, I was standing up, looking through a telescope, I could see there was a small island ahead, with palm trees growing on it, as we approached, I could make out Grandpa's figure waiting there for me. After disembarking, we greeted each other, it was great to see him.

Next, I found myself sitting at a long table and was surprised to see my Mum and Dad sat there, as well as

Grandma Tansley. I couldn't actually see anyone else, but sensed that all my relatives were there and knew there were no spare places at the table.

I noticed a chocolate cake, (my favourite), covered in white icing, with a cherry on the top, it had been placed on an ornate glass cake stand. I felt there was lots of food, although again I couldn't see it, but it smelt good and amongst these delicious smells was the smell of wine. We lifted our glasses to toast each other.

It was a party, as you have probably guessed and I could hear the cheers, the chatter and the laughing. How wonderful to join a spirit party on Christmas Day, I was beside myself with joy.

A Christmas cracker appeared in front of me, it took some pulling with an unseen spirit, however it eventually broke along the centre. A piece of paper floated from it, up to my face. It read: WE WOULD LIKE TO GIVE YOU A SURPRISE! (And they sure did.)

I found myself sitting in front of a very large box; it was as tall as me! The box was nicely wrapped in Christmas wrapping paper, tied up with a red ribbon, which was finished off in a lovely big bow. I unwrapped it eagerly revealing a nicely decorated box, with a hinged lid. I lifted the lid and to my surprise, out sprung an enormous Jack-in-a-box, not quite what I had expected, but it made me laugh.

Apparently, it was time to go and I found myself at the back of a speed boat, speeding through the water, waving good bye to everyone on the shore. I thanked them all for such a lovely party and felt so honoured that my spirit relatives had visited me on Christmas Day.

Grandpa has even been with me in church. I was sitting in the congregation one day, when I could feel his presence. Then, he began to tug my hair at the back, I had a hard time trying to stop myself from laughing out loud.

The medium on the platform turned her attention to me at this point and said that a man had joined her. He was of slim build and about six foot tall and very much a joker and a prankster. Yes, that was certainly a good description of my Grandpa! She described him walking with me, when I was a child, near cliffs in Yorkshire and said he was telling her that he had watched me grow up and is around me a great deal. He ended by sending his love. It's lovely to hear from him through someone else, it confirms my experiences and I am very grateful to him.

Sometimes, after I have done a service, he will come through. I remember one time, seeing the Statue of Liberty slugging back a bottle of alcohol and I knew it was him, having a laugh. There were also lots of men in the boat with me at the time, dressed in old-fashioned clothes drinking and being very merry.

Much later along my spiritual path, I held Awareness Classes for a group of people. On that day I had been teaching them about the seven main chakras of the body, using a small plastic skeleton to identify their positions. I had left it lying on the arm of the sofa, everyone had departed for home and I had gone into the kitchen to wash up the mugs, we always finished with a drink and refreshments at the end of the class.

When I returned into the lounge, the skeleton was sitting upright on the floor about half a metre from the sofa, its legs straight out in front of it with its feet turned outwards, the arms were straight with the hands flat on the floor keeping it upright. It made me laugh out loud to see it there, I knew my Grandpa was responsible. The chance of it landing in that position was very unlikely. My Grandpa is definitely a practical joker and I love him for it.

He doesn't always act the goat though, sometimes he helps to convey messages from the spirit world. Once I was paddling my canoe, when ahead of me, I could see Grandpa standing on an island, calmly lighting his pipe. My canoe drew up alongside the island and I stepped out to join him. He handed me a glass vial, cylindrical in shape, with gold ends.

Curious about what might be inside, I took off one of the gold ends. I peeped inside and saw a rolled-up piece of paper, gently taking it out and unrolling it, I found that it was a message for me. At the top in large letters, I read: WE WISH YOU WELL. Underneath there were three columns of signatures. Unfortunately, they were too vague to make out individual names, but I really appreciated the message and thanked them all for it.

Grandpa was there for me again one day, when I was quite shattered having done too much the day before. During meditation, I could feel his presence through the tightening of my throat. I paddled to an island in my canoe, Grandpa was waiting for me again and helped me out onto land.

I spotted a deckchair and decided to relax in it. The vast ocean was glistening in front of me, the scene was calm and mesmerising and bright sun beams bathed my face in the still air. I began to feel myself relaxing deeply and asked for my energy levels to be restored.

Gradually, as I sat there soaking up the sun and the calming view, I became re- energised, ready to start the chores again, coming out of meditation the energy and tranquillity remained.

Following another service, Grandpa began tightening my throat, the signal for me to go into meditation. I found myself in my canoe as usual, approaching an island, I landed the canoe and stepped onto land, in front of me was a forest of palm trees. I began to walk through them and after walking a short distance, I could see a long flight of stone steps, which I ascended, they seemed to go on for ever and a couple of times I had to stop for a breather and looked up to see how far I still had to go. When I finally reached the top, there were huge dark wooden doors with round brass handles in front of me.

I opened these huge doors with ease, inside there were rows of long tables, people whom I had never seen before sat around them and they all turned to look at me. I wasn't quite sure what to do, so I walked to the front of that great hall. I could hear lots of bells ringing, then noticed that they were all hung around the room. The magnificent hall was also decorated with different coloured balloons and bunting which moved slightly from the vibration of the bells.

The sound of party trumpets began to fill the air and once I had reached the front of the hall, I saw there was a two-tier cake on a small wooden table. On top of the cake stood a pyramid supported by four pillars. Strangely, bells hung from the base of the pyramid. I could hear, "Well done!" After which, I was given a glass of wine and toasted.

Everyone in the room started to sing the song, "For she's a jolly good fellow." I was quite moved by all this praise and attention. I thought to myself, that my Dad may have engineered this as he had often started singing that song at family weddings and everyone used to join in with him. I thanked everyone for such a lovely party.

Later, I realized that the bell theme for the party had been very appropriate, as Prince William and Catherine, the Duchess of Cambridge had just had their third child, Prince Louis and the bells of Westminster Cathedral had rung out to celebrate.

I remember not getting the buzz, I usually get after giving another service, probably because the message I was giving to the last lady was not being accepted, there seemed to be a number of "No" answers. A medium's nightmare, it can be very off putting. Luckily, a lady sat behind her said that she could take everything.

The next day during meditation, my oar became very long, moving about erratically, leaving my hand

and cork-screwing into the air towards the bright light of the sun. I was being told that mediumship is not straight forward, it has many twists and turns. It is forever a learning curve.

Yet another party after a service, I found I was holding a long paddle, signalling that the spirits were pleased with me. Despite the length of the paddle, I managed to make strokes in the water and propel the canoe forwards, Grandpa was with me.

I reached land and a large brown bear held onto the paddle, to gently pull me out of the canoe. I walked up to a castle and on the parapet, I could see medieval soldiers standing to attention, the chain-mail of their uniforms glinting in the sun. As I approached the magnificently carved wooden doors, they opened automatically. A lady with dark long wavy hair stood inside, she was wearing a full length light blue dress. She hastily took my hand and pulled me quickly down the long corridor to a room, the doors of which were already open wide, allowing me to see tables arranged in a circle. Many people were sitting around the outside of this circle of tables.

On entering the room, the lady in the blue dress disappeared and in the centre of the circle stood a three-tier cake on a little table. An ornamental prancing white horse was standing on top and the cake which was covered in glistening white icing.

I glanced around the tall circular room, the walls were made of stone and about two metres from the floor, there were recesses in the wall in which soldiers were standing, clad in chain-mail, like those soldiers standing on the parapet, wearing metal helmets with nose guards. In perfect unison they raised their long brass trumpets into the air, flags drooping from them and they began to play a fanfare. I could hear clapping and the chink of wine glasses. I was truly overcome by their kindness, giving me yet another party to celebrate my success at a service.

One of Grandpa's most memorable visits however, came two days before Christmas in 2018. My mother had packed boxes for us all, including the grandchildren before her passing, these boxes were full of family heirlooms. Fortunately for me, my eldest daughter didn't want hers, they didn't mean much to her and she didn't have the space to keep them. It was like Christmas Day for me, unpacking the box, full of what seemed to me wonderful treasures, some of which I had never seen before.

It contained an old family album, with pictures of many relatives whom I knew of, but had never seen. I was thrilled to bits when I glanced at my great grandfather's photo, he had been a master shoe maker. I had found this out when I had studied my ancestral tree, a few years prior. He had been to St Louis in America, the shoe capital of the world at the time, in order to improve his skills.

One night when falling asleep, I saw a very elegant pair of ladies' brown shoes come into my mind. They were very unusual as the upper shoe was made of tapestry, woven in different muted colours. I had never seen such unusual shoes before. I heard a voice say, "Walk tall with confidence." I feel it was probably him.

Back in the box, I found my parent's silver serviette rings and some of my mother's dress jewellery, amongst which was a ring supporting a translucent amber stone. It was quite significant, as prior to receiving this box, I had seen a vision of this ring.

Most exciting of all in the box, was my Grandpa's RAMC (Royal Army Medical Core) badge from the First World war and his ARP (Air Raid Precautions) badge from WW11. I was delighted to own some of his precious possessions, things he had actually held in his hand and cherished.

A few weeks later, he started to tighten my throat, I had to keep him waiting for three quarters of an hour as I was watching a programme and wanted to see the ending.

He waited patiently and when I was finally tuned in, I could see a man and wife, not actually in focus, but they were holding a baby. I mentioned it to my sister later, because I felt it was her youngest daughter who was pregnant. My sister already knew about the pregnancy, but had been asked to keep it a secret for a couple of months, so denied it at that time. However, a few months later she apologised for not being truthful and verified the good news. Eventually, my niece gave birth to a healthy baby boy.

My meditation didn't end there, I saw my Grandpa standing on the semi-circular terrace surrounded by an ornate balustrade where I have met him many times before. He was busy shaking hands with a group of women dressed in 1940's clothes and I knew these were women who he had rescued from the rubble, after the terrible bombing raids by the Germans in Birmingham, during the second World War.

After this, I was shown the devastation in the city. I saw lots of houses with only a corner of the building left standing, there were mounds of rubble everywhere and isolated fires burning around the city. A policeman came up the road on horseback and there was a donkey carrying rubble on its back.

I saw a poor old lady laid face down in the mud pinned down by a wooden joist. I could make out her grey hair tied at the back of her head in a bun. She had passed away, unfortunately.

Grandpa finally showed me a glimpse of him wearing his first World War uniform, standing there proudly, for what looked like a photography session.

I was grateful for seeing these images, it gave me a better insight into the terrible situation everyone found themselves, during those dreadful days of war. It made me feel very proud of my Grandpa, for having helped all those people after the air raids, often putting his own life at risk, by entering unstable buildings and walking over uneven slippery mounds of rubble, in order to find people. I feel so much closer to him now, knowing what he had to go through.

A few days later, he was indicating that I should go into meditation again. I did so and he showed me a picture of himself and said, "I love you," then appeared in profile smoking his pipe.

I told him that I liked his silver-plated matchstick containers which had also arrived with his other personal items in that box. "I liked them too." He agreed.

My Grandpa has also been my alarm clock!

I had decided to meditate prior to setting off for a service one time and didn't want to set my alarm, as the shrill bleeping can bring me out of my trance-like state and send me almost into shock, when I'm so deep in meditation. Before meditating, I had asked my Grandpa to let me know when it was one o'clock. After some time in meditation, I felt my throat tightening intensely. I opened my eyes to find it was precisely one o'clock.

It was not the only occasion that spirit made me aware of the time. I was waking up one morning my eyes still closed, wondering how long it was until eight o'clock, when the alarm would go off. I distinctly heard a female voice say, "one minute." I sat up in a shot and glanced at my mobile phone, it was exactly 7.59 am. I have no idea who the lady was, but it proves that spirit people are around us all the time.

Grandpa helps me in other ways too, I have an elderly friend called Janice, who lives on her own. I visit her regularly to have a chat and on a nice day, I often drive her to a local cafe for a drink and a catch-up on our news.

On the way to her house, the car was stifling, the weather being so hot, I decided to lower the passenger side window, to let in some fresh air. When Janice sat in the passenger seat, she found it a bit too draughty with the window open. I pressed the button numerous times to close it, but nothing happened and I had to park the car in the carpark with the window still down.

After our cup of coffee and a chat, I dropped Janice off at her house and decided to go to the car repair centre on the way home to get it fixed. It was important that I got it fixed as the next day, I was due to visit my cousin in Wales and wouldn't have been able to leave the car anywhere with its window open. I came to the cross roads where one direction took me home and the other direction took me to the car repair centre. I had to stop there for a while and wait for the traffic to clear before turning.

Grandpa came around me very strongly tightening my throat, I felt I needed to try the switch again and to my surprise the window closed without any problem, I was able to go straight home without taking a detour and it has worked ever since.

Another strange thing has happened a couple of times now, I've been watching a programme that I have been particularly interested in and felt my Grandpa come around me. The next thing I knew on both occasions there had been a loss of time, about ten minutes in all, my programmes had finished and the next ones had started. Grandpa was still with me on both occasions, when I became aware of my surroundings again.

I asked him, "Why have I lost ten minutes."

He replied, "Don't worry, I have done what I needed to do."

I have no idea what he needed to do, but I trust him implicitly and know he would never do me any harm. I'm for ever grateful to my Grandpa for everything he does for me and I thoroughly enjoy his visits.

Chapter 9

Isaac

Grandpa was around me when I went into meditation and strangely enough, I found myself in a dodgem car. It was the shape and colour of a ladybird, quite significant as I had seen a ladybird that morning whilst gardening.

The dodgem car was floating automatically down a stream, without any effort from me because I hadn't been given a paddle. I arrived at a large lake surrounded by majestic mountains, rising high into the sky.

At the far end of the lake, I could see a gap in the mountains. The dodgem car made its way across the lake to this gap, which led out to sea. I could see a beautiful red sunset on the horizon, which began to emit a brilliant white light, at the same time the moon rose in the darkening sky and it too sent out tremendous white light which shone over me.

Just then a helicopter flew overhead and I could see a rope ladder being lowered, an elderly man descended into my dodgem car. He was wearing a black cloak and wore a band of gold across his forehead. His long white beard fell down to his waist and ended in a point. I asked him his name, he replied," Isaac."

I remembered my first Awareness Class teacher, Mary telling me of a man with the same name and description and she told me he was my philosophy guide. This had been two years previous and I had completely forgotten about him until that point in time.

The scene changed and I found myself in a cluttered room, everywhere I looked there were stacks and stacks of books, big ones and small ones, all really old with dusty faded covers. Isaac was sitting at a dark wooden table busy writing in an old-fashioned book using a quill. He didn't stop what he was doing, but said, "I will give you everything that you need to know."

Grandpa had been close around me to give me reassurance. I thanked them both. Isaac had come just at the right time, obviously planned by him, as I had been asked to give a Divine Service a few weeks later as I have mentioned in an earlier chapter and would be required to give up to fifteen minutes of philosophy.

Over the next few days, Isaac had put into my mind the title, "Trust in Spirit," and ideas of what to talk about, as I hadn't a clue.

A few days before the service arrived, I meditated and found myself in my canoe on the lake surrounded by mountains and made my way to the sea through the gap once again. There on the horizon the sun was steadily rising and as it rose it started to emit brilliant white light which washed over me, as it had done several times before and I fused with this light.

My Dad had also joined me, he was sitting at the front of the canoe, on a chair wearing a shirt and tie with a cerise coloured V-neck sweater. He was smiling at me and I asked him to send me good luck. He said, "You don't need it. I am very proud of you." On saying these words, he disappeared. I was elated and much more confident that the service would go OK.

During the service, I gave the philosophy on "Trust in Spirit" incorporating the ideas that Isaac had given me. Thankfully, the congregation enjoyed it and I had good feedback from everyone.

A month or so later, I was watching the television waiting for the weather forecast. It had been very dry and I wanted to know if rain was due to save me from having to water the garden. My throat started tightening, a sure sign that Grandpa wanted me to go into meditation. I kept the television on, as I really did not want to miss the weather forecast, but was amazed at what happened next.

I found myself floating at breakneck speed down a tunnel which twisted and turned. I was going so fast I gasped and felt quite dizzy, at the end of the tunnel, I floated out into a black abyss. Initially, I thought Grandpa had done this for me, to make me relax as I was anxious about a friend of mine who had become quite ill. I did in fact relax and felt quite calm and serene, when suddenly, a bright white light came towards me and as it came closer, I could make out the figure of Isaac, my philosophy guide literally glowing with brightness. As he approached, he said, "Don't make it up, I will help you."

This made sense to me, I had been pondering about philosophy subjects to talk about during future Divine Services. It seems that Isaac was going to give me the subjects and help me with the content as well.

It was then that I found myself in a large room full of bookshelves, starting from the floor reaching up as far as the ceiling, they were all ladened with old books of all sizes. I noticed Isaac perched high upon a ladder leaning against the shelving. He seemed to be looking for a specific book and having found it he opened it declaring, "It's all here." Apparently, all the philosophy that I required was written in that book.

Isaac stepped down from the ladder and came across the room to where I was standing and handed me the large book and as I took hold of it, I could feel its heavy weight and could see it in much more detail. It had a great number of pages inside a thick dark green cover which felt rough to the touch, I could actually feel the waft and the weft of the material that had been used. Two rounded bands of orange-brown coloured wood, were attached equidistant from each other on the cover, these bands continued around the large spine of the book in a curving fashion and continued along the lower cover.

When I opened the book, there was page after page of printed words, with no sign of any pictures, photos or drawings. I thanked Isaac for the book and came out of meditation, in no doubt that Isaac was getting me ready to give more philosophy.

He came disguised one day. I found myself in my canoe with a cloaked man, wearing a wide brimmed hat, sitting at the other end paddling the canoe, when I asked him why I wasn't holding the paddle he said, "To give you a rest."

The canoe suddenly took a horizontal dive down a waterfall and came to rest in the calm waters below. At this point I asked him who he was as I still hadn't recognised him. He declared, "Isaac."

I've had my paddle taken over before and the spirit person paddling the canoe has taken me through a challenging patch on my spiritual path.

In this case, I was starting to give philosophy at Divine Services. I had not been brought up as a spiritualist and had never been to a spiritualist church until a few years prior, so hadn't been familiar with the giving of philosophy. During the last couple of years however, I had tried to attend as many services as possible to learn about it.

Many mediums can give philosophy on the platform without any preparation. Their philosophy guides tell them what to say as they go along, I find this remarkable. Others talk about something that may have happened that day, to include in their philosophy. I always admire those who have not prepared anything and can talk fluently for ten to fifteen minutes about a significant topic, often linked to the chairperson's address.

I seem to work a bit differently; my philosophy guide often gives me a subject to talk about, after that I receive flashes of information to give to the congregation, other times I am drawn to a book, or information on the computer.

One day, I saw Isaac seated at his large wooden table busy writing with his quill, without looking up or a word from me, he said, "Forgiveness." Clearly, the subject for my next philosophy.

Out of the blue, a few days later, I was attending my art class in the village, when a lady I hardly knew approached me. She said, "I know you're into psychic things. I thought you might like this," handing me a paper-back book. She went on to explain that she had bought it in a charity shop and had read it, and enjoyed it, but didn't want to hold onto it.

I thanked her and when I got home and looked through it, there was a whole chapter on "forgiveness", including a story, to give an example. I was very pleased, spirit work in such mysterious ways. Naturally, this was my topic at the next Divine Service and a few people came up afterwards, to tell me that they had enjoyed the service.

Isaac came a few days before I was due at Cleveley's Spiritualist Church. I found myself standing in a library, in a circular room full of hundreds of books which were neatly standing on shelves that began almost at floor level and went all the way up to the ceiling.

I recognised his unkempt long grey hair, his gold band and long dark-coloured cloak, He clambered up a ladder to reach for a particular book and brought it back to where I was standing. He opened it and flicked through the pages, until he found the right page. He then pointed to a word halfway down the page on the righthand side. I leaned in to have a better look, the word said, "opportunity," in black print. My topic for the next philosophy. I thanked him.

During the next few months, I gave philosophy at several services. Isaac had given me the titles and had helped me with the content.

Ramanov had joined me in my canoe after the last of these services and I found myself paddling backwards down a waterfall, I've never gone backwards before and questioned Ramanov on this. He replied, "Because you are doing the same as at Fleetwood." I knew exactly what he meant, that day I was giving a Divine Service in Blackpool and had decided to give the same philosophy, as I had given at the Spiritualist Church at Fleetwood a week or so before.

Ramanov definitely thought I was going backwards in my spiritual development as each philosophy should be different and it made me feel quite guilty. He wasn't too cross with me though, as he changed into my father, who gave me reassurance and I could feel my spirit mother stroking my left hand, as she often does when she comes around me.

After the service, a man had approached with his wife, they were both mediums and thanked me for his message and a lovely service. I had spoken to them before after a service and we began talking again. I mentioned that I had a philosophy guide now, called Isaac, who wore a gold band around his head. The husband of the couple told me that the philosophers in ancient times wore gold bands on their heads for two reasons. They thought that the gold would stimulate their brains and secondly, they believed that the gold band improved connection to the spirit world. He added that generally, it was those philosophers with gold bands who were connected to royalty. I was truly honoured to have such a high-status philosopher guiding me.

Isaac often came to give me encouragement, as well as everyone else. I saw him in my vision one day, hunched over a table writing with a quill by candle light. He rarely looks up at me and this occasion was no exception. He just said, "You will achieve great things."

I'm sure he will always be there for me each time I'm asked to do a Divine Service, giving me guidance on the specific philosophy that he wants me to talk about.

Chapter **10**

Ismos

Ismos came out of the blue one day. The spirit world never seems to let one know when a new spirit guide is about to take over. In fact, I heard a medium on the platform one day, announce in the middle of a message, that he had a new guide who had just appeared. Each one works slightly differently and I've found that the signs and symbols that they give can differ slightly and it can take a little while to get used to them.

As I said, Ismos just appeared one day when I was meditating. He suddenly manifested at the other end of the canoe, bare-chested wearing a headband supporting a red-tipped white feather standing vertically at the back of his head. I could feel Grandpa's presence too. I greeted the Indian and asked his name, he replied, "Ismos," or something very similar. Straight afterwards, before I had chance to confirm his name, he declared that he was my new spirit guide.

Naturally, I was quite surprised, it was totally unexpected and not a good time as I was going to do platform mediumship at a church in few days time. Needless to say, my guide looked after me and all went well.

It was a few weeks later before he appeared again and he let me know that I would do well at the next two services coming up a few days later. His visits were very infrequent, perhaps he felt I'm well on my way and didn't need as much contact.

However, a few weeks later he appeared in my canoe, facing away from me with the paddle in his hand, negotiating the rapid river, we came to a waterfall and we went horizontally down it. Ismos skilfully edged the canoe around some boulders before we reached quieter water and took the bend to the left along the river. I felt my guide was about to steer me through some turbulent times and I thanked him for it.

It was then that my mother-in-law appeared in her mayoral robes and chain. She had also been a magistrate, very interested in keeping law and order in her home town and took her role very seriously.

She has appeared on a few occasions dressed like this, usually when there had been some sort of injustice, where the person was in fact innocent. In this instance, she had come through about a friend of mine, who used to live in Southport, he was a gardener for a slightly confused elderly man and had had been accused of stealing, consequently, he had been dismissed. My friend was very upset of course, but I trusted him, especially after having seen my mother-in-Law and so my friend started working for someone else that I knew, who lived much closer to his home, making it more convenient for him anyway.

As Ismos didn't visit very often, other spirit people came instead. One day, I saw several Indian Chiefs in another canoe going in the opposite direction. I asked them where they were going, one of them said, "We are going to war!"

"Can I come?" I enquired.

"Stay where you are," they replied.

My meditation continued and I saw a gap in the mountains ahead and paddled through towards the sea. A white brilliant light issued from the sun overhead and as I have done many times before, I fused with it, I was being prepared for the service in Blackpool, taking place in a couple of days.

A few days later, I heard about a scallop fishing dispute in the English Channel involving the British and French fishermen. This was named: The Great Scallop War which occurred on 28th August 2018. I wondered if this had been the war that the Indians were going to. Three trawlers and two boats got damaged, as far as I am aware no one was killed.

I have had visions of spirits going to war before. They are there to give healing to the injured and help those that are killed allowing them to make their transition into the spirit world.

A few days later, Ismos appeared in my canoe again, I was to give a Divine Service at the St. Anne's Spiritual Church a couple of days ahead. I recognised him at once by his bare chest and red tipped white feather in his headband. He put a kind of musical pipe to his mouth. I couldn't hear any sound, but he was apparently calling the troops, for boat loads of Indians arrived and I could hear them all shouting, "We're here to help." My heart melted, I'm so grateful for their continued help and support.

A few weeks later, Ismos joined me in my canoe, eating meat from a large bone. I asked him the significance of this and he replied, "I'm feasting, celebrating, you will do so well."

I was booked to do two services within days of each other and asked if I would do OK at the second service, at Preston Ethical Spiritualist Church. He stopped eating and looked at me saying, "You will do even better."

A day later Ismos visited me again. He stood up and threw an arrow into the air, propeller blades appeared around the arrowhead and the arrow began to spin very quickly, it continued in a straight-line trajectory and I never saw it fall.

I find that my guides often give me puzzles like this, upon reflection I feel he was trying to tell me that my mediumship had gathered pace and would go on and on. So far thankfully, it has.

They also give me encouragement in the most peculiar ways. When setting off to do a service at Fleetwood Spiritualist Church, one time, I switched on the car radio, surprised to hear the song, "Don't worry about a thing." I smiled for I know that they are around me all the time.

Another time I was a little despondent, wondering whether I was good enough, lack of confidence rearing its ugly head again. Ismos was there rowing my canoe instead of paddling it. I was standing on the bank watching, wondering what was going to happen. He said, "I'm taking over."

I was quite concerned when I saw the canoe starting to sink, until I could only see his head above the water. Now I knew why I had been left standing on the bank. Gradually, he surfaced, still sitting in the canoe and set off rowing again, as if nothing had happened.

I feel he was telling me that the journey of mediumship can become quite overwhelming at times and hence the sinking feeling, but as he demonstrated, things will improve and I will set off again as before.

His encouragement had worked and I had very good feedback from the next service at which I spent ten minutes or so talking about, "Responsibility."

It didn't go unnoticed by Ismos, as the next morning, I was barely awake when I felt myself being dropped into my canoe. Ismos was already sitting there at the other end. He kindly said, "You did well my friend." I thanked him and he disappeared.

It isn't always my guides who prepare me for a service. I was honoured by a medieval king visiting me in my canoe during meditation one day. He wore a gold crown, other than that he wasn't richly dressed at all, just clad in a brown cloak. The paddle became an arrow and he held it pointing to the sky. A very bright white beam of light came down over him, he kept the arrow aloft and disappeared into the light. The bright light started to surround me and I realized that I too was fusing with it.

It isn't only prior to the services when I seem to fuse with the light. I was due to go to a person's house to give an evening of mediumship. Whilst meditating in my canoe that day, I saw a tall conical-shaped mountain capped with snow in the far distance. It turned into a pyramid, which was significant as I had watched a programme on TV the day before, about pyramids. I found myself standing on the top of this pyramid and saw a shaft of bright white light descending from the sky, engulfing me and like many times before, I seemed to fuse with it.

The hostess, that evening was very impressed with the readings, especially when I described her own aunty, first as she was in her old age before she passed and then, in her long white wedding dress on her wedding day, I also described her nicely styled dark hair and that she was holding a cascading bouquet of beautiful flowers. I could "see" this in a framed photo of her. The hostess, immediately went to fetch it, to prove what I had said.

Another participant, a young lady was basically told off by her spirit grandmother. (Spirit relatives often speak their mind and will tell someone off if they see fit to do so.) I had described her and the young lady knew which grandma it was. Her gran told her quite firmly, to be happy with what she had. I learned later that this young lady was never happy with what she had and was always wanting more and more things from relatives.

I had another spirit telling her daughter off, during a private reading once. She was quite a feisty woman who had come through wagging her finger, just as she used to do when she was on the earth plane. I had a terrible urge to wag my finger at her too, put on me by this spirit lady. Once I realised what I was doing, I had to actually hold my finger still to stop it wagging at her. Her mother was very cross. She said, "I have done my job, it's time to do yours!" Then, in my vision she stomped off.

I didn't want the sitter to go home feeling unloved by her Mum. I told her that it was because her mother loved her very much that she had come to tell her to move on with her life. Her mother had passed away sometime previously and she admitted that she wasn't able to let go. She understood that her mother was telling her in no uncertain terms that it was now time, to let go.

Ismos would also comfort me, he sat in my canoe one day wearing only a leather skirt around his waist, his chest was bare as usual and for the first time I could see that his legs and feet were bare as well. In his right hand he held a tomahawk. An estranged relative who prefers not to have any contact with several members of the family, had come into my thoughts many times around that time. "Don't give up hope for her," he said gently. I asked if we would be reunited soon. He replied, "A long time yet." I sent my love to her. A few days later I was due to do another service, he said, "We will be with you." I thanked him.

Ismos has also guided other people. Joan and Cecily, my dear friends who lost their cat if you remember, were travelling from their new home in the south to see me in Preston. They had already phoned to say they would be late as they had been caught up in a traffic jam. I asked my guide to bring them safely to my house without getting lost, as they always seemed to miss their way. When they finally arrived, they remarked that for once they hadn't got lost. They told me that they just seemed to know which way to go. I told them about my request to Ismos.

Ismos continued to guide me and about this time, I was asked to go and give one-to-one spiritual readings at a spiritualist church. Ismos was with me in my canoe when I went into meditation. My oar changed into a gigantic fork and I heard him say, "Have a stab at it." Then, I found myself in a clearing in the woods, six North American Indian women, dressed in Indian tunics were holding hands and they began to dance around me.

The readings went well and I had good feedback. Unfortunately, I never remember much of the information that I give when I'm working, I'm in a kind of dream state. I just remember snippets, often the information is given in movie form, for instance the spirit friends and relatives who come through may be busy doing something. The ladies are sometimes baking or hanging out the washing or typing if they had been a typist.

The men maybe gardening if that's what they liked to do before passing over, or tinkering with a bike or car, going for a walk or fishing if those were their hobbies. They often show me what kind of work they used to do too and I may see a postman on his rounds or a bus driver driving his bus.

Quite often both man and wife will come together and I can describe them both in detail and often give the relationship that the sitter had with them.

Many of the things that are shown to me are symbolic, for example, if I see a person trapped in a hole, this often signifies that they are in some way trapped in their own lives, perhaps in an unhappy marriage or a job that doesn't suit them, and they don't know how to go forward, of course the spirits are there to help.

It is not always my guides who present themselves in my meditations as I have said before. On one occasion, I was in my canoe, it was cold and dark, when a man who I had never seen before, appeared at the other end of the boat. He was about thirty years of age; the sleeves of his shirt were rolled up and he wore a working man's waistcoat and trousers.

He was holding a huge wooden object resembling a fork and banging the middle prong with a wooden mallet. I asked him what he was doing, without looking my way he said, "Making something." This reply wasn't much help of course, so I enquired if it was for me, "When it's finished." At this point he handed it to me, the prongs began to burn and large flames rose up from each prong, "It's to light your way," he added.

Not realising what I was supposed to do with it, I started to blow out the middle flame. He hastily said, "Don't blow it out, you will need it to light your way." I thanked him.

When I had first gone into the meditation, I could see a spur of land in the night sky and a huge fire was issuing out of it. I remember thinking that I hoped there wouldn't be another fire somewhere.

Six days later, the news reported a substantial fire at Chester Zoo and unfortunately several animals had lost their lives.

Spirit priests have visited me too on a few occasions. Sometimes I have seen them walking around the inside of our circle during Development Class or the Open Circle giving us all a blessing. They have come during my meditations too. One time, A priest wearing a dog collar was playing a guitar. I asked him who he was and why he had come, he was quite chirpy and told me that he was a friend and had come to make me happy. I thanked him.

A few days later, I found myself sitting in the guest seat of my canoe and a large muscular man, wearing a red bandana with white polka-dots, had taken my place at the other end of the canoe. He also wore an open-necked white shirt and brown waistcoat. Scanning his body, I could see thick brown loose trousers and heavy high ankle boots. He said nothing, but began to paddle a short distance down the river, coming to a standstill on the edge of a waterfall. We perched there rather precariously.

Spirits have taken over the paddling of my canoe before and paddled me to a waterfall keeping me teetering on the edge. This usually happens when I'm going through a challenging time and sure enough, Christmas was looming once again, it isn't the best time of year for me. All my groups and classes shut down for a fortnight over the Christmas period and it can be a bit boring for me, when the meals and parties are over.

The next day, I meditated again and there I was still balanced on the edge of the waterfall, just like the day before, with the same man sat in my seat. This time he was wearing a black eye patch over his eye. I was a little afraid as his attire resembled that of a pirate and I wasn't sure what he was up to. I asked my guide, Ismos for more protection and in a flash the big muscular man changed into a petite woman in her twenties, wearing the same type of clothes, without the eye patch. I felt a little easier. We went gracefully, horizontally down the waterfall to the bottom, where the water was totally smooth, not a ripple to be seen.

The spirits helped me through the Christmas period, things weren't as bad as I thought they would be and life went back to normal again afterwards. Ismos didn't stay long as my spirit guide and as usual didn't give me any warning of a new guide taking his place. I never saw him again.

Chapter 11

Ignato

___

I had had a heavy sensation in my chest for several hours, Grandpa started tightening my throat, a sign to go into meditation as there was something important to be told. I was busy at the time and kept him waiting for twenty minutes.

When I finally meditated, I found myself as usual in my canoe and at the other end was sat an elderly North American Indian with a cloak was wrapped tightly around him. His headdress was quite different to those I had seen before and was decorated with alternating red and black tipped feathers. The lower part of them were white decorated in a fine black pattern, it looked like the pattern had been painted on for extra decoration.

He said that he was called Ignuga, or something like that, I couldn't hear his name clearly, but before I had the chance to ask him to clarify it, he continued, "I am your new spirit guide."

I could feel Grandpa still around me and I welcomed the Indian. He went on to say, "I have rules." Feeling curious, I naturally asked him what these rules were.

He replied, "I want you to obey my commands."

I told him that, "It is free-will."

"Then, I will not speak to you."

Mediums have always told me that if the spirits give you a message to give to someone or tell you to do something, it is entirely up to the individual whether they act upon it. I asked him what the other rules were. He replied, "To sleep when I tell you to."

Sleep for me had been an issue at this time, I was finding it hard to sleep for very long at night and consequently was always tired in the daytime, so I felt it was significant that he should bring this up. I thanked him and at the same time gave a deep involuntary sigh and as I did so the heaviness in my chest evaporated, I feel he made this happen.

His rule, "To sleep when I tell you to," became apparent later and I feel this new guide came to help me through an illness. Continuing my meditation, I saw a young Indian boy standing up at the other end of my canoe, holding a blow pipe in his mouth.

Looking upwards towards the sky, I could see a small Blue Tit flying around and hoped that the Indian boy wasn't going to kill it. I wanted to distract him and told him how beautiful I thought it was. He turned to look at me.

At that moment, I could hear Ignuga's voice coming from nowhere, "You are beautiful." This was very kind of him and very significant, as recently I had told a friend about a boyfriend, who I had gone out with, many years previously, who had said that I was very plain and not very beautiful. Thankfully, I'm not a vain person and I'm quite comfortable with my appearance. I told him that I was beautiful on the inside instead, I believe that I am a good person and try to help others whenever I can. I think beauty on the inside is far more valuable than beauty on the outside, but I thanked Ignuga for his compliment anyway.

At the beginning of the meditation, I was very tired and lacked energy and now I felt fully energised. I came out of the meditation not sure if Ignuga was my guide, as I hadn't had one who had told me to obey his rules before.

An hour later, Grandpa came around me, I went back into meditation. He didn't appear, but I recognised his voice, "Believe, it is true you have a new spirit guide." Not sure of his name, I felt it was the perfect opportunity to enquire if I had heard it correctly. Grandpa quickly clarified it, telling me that he was called," Ignato."

Now I was certain of his proper name.

My Grandpa left me standing in a clearing in a wood surrounded by a circle of Indian girls holding hands. They were all dressed in brown tunics, with nothing on their feet and dancing merrily around me. I always feel honoured and moved when I have so much attention from the spirit world.

A few days later, I'm back in my canoe with Ignato sat at the other end. He changed into a female and shrunk to baby-size and landed in my lap. A sign that a baby is due and later I found out that it was one of my six nieces who was pregnant.

Ignato appeared again to tell me, "I will teach you many things." I thanked him and asked him if I would do well at the Portland Street Church Service in a week's time. "You will do so well," he replied.

A three-tiered cake appeared with half a dozen lit candles on the top. I asked him why he had given me this lovely cake because I hadn't yet done the service. "It's for your success." I thanked him again.

Next, I found myself standing on grass, no longer in the canoe. A blond-haired lady in a long white dress floated towards me, she was holding a lit candle in an ornate candlestick. The light coming from the candle became intensely brighter and brighter, as she floated towards me, naturally, I thought I would be fusing with the light, but didn't. I could hear Ignato saying, "You don't need to fuse with the light anymore."

Strangers continued to visit me in meditation and I saw a North American Indian sitting in my canoe sometime later. He wore a light-coloured tunic with trousers and on his head was a lovely headdress of black-tipped feathers. He introduced himself as Brown Bear, after we had exchanged greetings. I asked him why he had come to visit me. "To give you best wishes for your mediumship." I thanked him and thought about the kindness of everyone in the spirit world and how lucky I am to experience these things.

Not long afterwards another North American Indian came to visit me. He made himself comfortable at the other end of my canoe. Once he was seated, I could see him properly and admired his beautiful headdress, the feathers were white at the base, turning to red in the middle, changing to black at the tip. I asked him his name, with no reply.

"Please speak to me," I urged.

"What do you want me to say?"

"Anything,"

Just at that moment, a carved wooden stick floated into view. He caught it and handed it to me. I took a few seconds to examine it and noticed an expertly carved head at one end. I thanked him and asked him why he had given it to me. "To help you walk along your mediumship path." He stated. I was very grateful to him.

On the bank to the left of us I could see a bonfire, its flames were leaping into the sky and several Indians were dancing around it, chanting as they moved their bodies this way and that, swaying their arms above their heads.

The wooden carving must have helped when I gave a reading two days later. It's not often that I remember the messages and readings that I give, but I seemed to remember a great deal of this one. The person receiving the message was called Valerie, who has given me permission to write about it.

The reading started with a small rounded lady appearing in my vision, who had grey permed hair,

I felt she was a lovely kind lady, but a bit shy. It was her spirit mother. Valerie confirmed this. She had brought with her a tortoise-shell cat with a white patch on its front, which Valerie remembered. She smiled when I described a brown dog, who had been in the family for several years. A budgie was also flying around in my vision and that had been a pet as well and I saw a tropical bird on the earth plane and she could place that too.

I was shown someone washing windows, Valerie had been busy doing that in the morning, before she came to see me. In my vision, I saw that she was reading a book at that time and she confirmed this.

A man who passed in his seventies, average height with a bit of a paunch joined me. He was quite light-hearted and funny. Valerie agreed it was her brother. He proceeded to put his finger in his cheek and pulled it out, making a popping sound. She laughed and said, "He was always doing that to make people laugh." He started to eat a huge cheese sandwich, apparently his favourite and then I saw him with several lollipops. Valerie said, "It was typical of him."

A vision of Morecombe Bay came into my head and Valerie said that the whole family had gone there on holiday in her youth. He gave several other childhood memories, one of which was a trip to a circus where there had been a small monkey waving a flag, dressed in a red waistcoat and a red fez. Another memory had been a visit to a zoo, where I saw large wrought iron gates surrounded by a decorative arch and at the top of the arch was the word, "Zoo" crafted in wrought iron too. Valerie hadn't thought about these trips for years, but remembered the monkey and the wrought iron gates too.

Next, I saw a celebratory toast was being made with two full wine glasses, clinking together. Valerie said it was her sister's birthday the following week. She could also take two birthday months and November as being significant as well.

I saw tears in my vision and heard her brother say, "Every cloud has a silver lining." She said there had been tears and agreed with what her brother had said. "There is apprehension about an appointment," her brother announced, she explained that it was regarding a friend of her partner, they had been talking about it that day. I saw a girl skipping, which signified that he would skip through it and it wouldn't be as bad as he thought it would be. A man who had taken his life by hanging himself came through and wanted her to know that he was alright. She remembered this man.

Her brother said, "There has been sadness, it takes time to heal and there is a need to forgive someone." Valerie explained that her brother had passed over in recent years and she still missed him very much. She added that there was definitely a certain relative whom she needed to forgive and she hoped that in time she would.

She thanked me for the reading and was glad that her mother and brother had come through. She felt grateful towards her brother for reminding her of all those wonderful memories that she had shared with him as a child. The session had made her feel quite happy and uplifted. I was glad to have helped her.

Between readings and messages, I continued to meditate. Ignato didn't visit me very often, but I was pleased to have other spirits join me during my meditations. I'm not always sitting in my canoe and on this particular occasion I was standing on the bank overlooking the river, four Indians and a sailor in uniform were sitting in a conical boat. It looked rather funny as they didn't seem to have any control of where they were going and were going round and round with the current, floating down the river. They sailed over the waterfall managing to keep upright, unfortunately, as they reached the water below, the sailor fell overboard, but a moment later, he was stood before me dripping wet saying, "I'm still living."

I took this symbolically to mean that terrible events may occur in one's life, but life goes on and one must accept them and move forward.

A few days later I had a similar vision during my meditation. I was busy paddling my canoe, when an Indian stood up at the other end, firstly playing a guitar which changed into bagpipes, followed by a violin. We suddenly went horizontally down a waterfall and crashed into the water below.

Unfortunately, I couldn't hang on and fell into the water. Soaked to the skin, I dragged myself back into the boat, luckily for me, I became an observer, watching myself fall into the water and dragging myself out. I find that my guides never let me actually experience things that may not be very nice. I became detached and saw the events unfolding instead.

These happenings were quite poignant of course at this time. My estranged relative's birthday was a couple of weeks ahead, it was going to be a difficult time for me, but the Indians clearly wanted me to move on and not dwell on the situation.

Soon after, I was visited by another Indian whom I had never seen before. His headdress was unusual all the feathers were totally black, held to the head band with red binding. He sat at the other end of the canoe and lit his long clay pipe. I welcomed him and asked him his name, again I didn't quite catch it, he may have said, "Souki" or something similar. He declared, "You are doing too much."

It was true, I had been very busy with everything and was feeling very tired. I asked, "Please let me do these next three services well and I won't do as many, all at once again."

I had volunteered to do two extra services, the mediums who had been booked for them had cancelled for various reasons and as well as these, I also had a service at Fleetwood, all within a few days of each other. He replied, "We will grant you that."

It was after the first service that another Indian probably in his forties, joined me in my canoe. He had a single red-tipped feather at the back of his head, tucked into his headband. He came with his guitar and began to play it, at the same time getting bigger and bigger. He said, "Cheer up,"

I was quite down as my mediumship at the last service hadn't been brilliant. Afterwards, the chairperson had said that several mediums had reported that the energies weren't very good in that community centre and they too had struggled with their messages.

Since that time, I have heard of a number of mediums who have had difficulty connecting with spirit whilst on the platform. One excellent medium had to ask the congregation to sing another hymn, in order to raise the energy vibrations inside the church, before the spirits connected with him.

People take it for granted that the spirits will always be there. A friend of mine gave the opening prayer and ten minutes of philosophy and when it was time for the communication part of the service, she couldn't connect to the spirit world. It must have been the worst moment of her life when she had to admit it. She told me later that there was no way that she could continue or even make it up. That would have been impossible. Thankfully, it rarely happens and it has never happened again to me.

Before my next service, I meditated and as usual found myself in my canoe, I asked to be taken to the lagoon surrounded by mountains where I have been several times before, it is very calm and tranquil there.

In an instant, I was in the middle of the lagoon, the boat standing still in the water. One by one Indians came to sit at the other end of the boat, Grandpa was there too. They took over the paddling of the boat. This has happened before when I have lost confidence in my mediumship, they take over, until my confidence is restored.

They took me to the gap in the mountains where the sea begins and there in front of us was an intense bright white light. The boat drifted towards it and I fused with the light. It has been sometime since they brought the light forward and I felt comforted.

It was only two days later, when I was astonished to see Ramanov in the boat. He was wearing his magnificent headdress and had taken over the paddling. I thought he had gone forever and I was overjoyed to see him. I found myself in the lagoon again with him, surrounded by the mountains.

He said, "Come my child be brave." He stood up and sang an Indian chant whilst playing a guitar. I joined in, I can't remember all the words now, but it ended in "Ya Ya."

He began to grow taller and taller at this point, I gave a heavy involuntary sigh, presumably letting go of my stress and as I did so, I grew taller and taller. He rowed us to the gap in the mountains, the bright white light appeared and I fused with it. He came the next day too, doing exactly the same thing, I grew taller and taller again, symbolically growing in confidence.

Happily, it worked, for my next service in Southport went well. The messages that I gave were all very humorous and everyone was laughing. The President approached me afterwards and told me that she had come to the church feeling quite low, but the service had cheered her up.

I didn't meditate for a couple of weeks, because I was so busy spring cleaning and sorting the garden after the winter season.

My next meditation was very different from normal. I was being led down a steep set of stone steps, making my way down a mountain. A Scottish piper in full regalia walked on in front of me, leading the way. Although he appeared to be playing his bagpipes, I couldn't actually hear them. We arrived at a small cove with a tiny beach, I recognised where I was, in front of me was the lagoon, surrounded by mountains.

"Where is my boat?" I asked.

Ignato's voice replied, "We are giving you a rest."

I decided to sit on the beach, relax and look at the wonderful scenery and I actually fell asleep.

It was quite significant that my guide wanted me to rest because I was feeling quite ill, having got a bit of a temperature, sore throat and low energy levels. Ignato's rule about sleeping, which he mentioned when we first met, began to make sense.

Five days later, I'm back in my canoe, the sides of which were quite high, a sign that the spirits were pleased with me, perhaps because I have done nothing but rest in the last few days. It's not like me to lounge around all day, but my poor energy levels didn't allow me to do much more than that.

At the other end of the canoe sat a cat, wearing a hat, playing a mournful tune on a violin. The spirits do this to me when I'm feeling sorry for myself, it makes me laugh. I have to admit that I had been feeling quite down, following my illness.

It was night time in the meditation and there was a full moon shining ahead. The canoe was gently bobbing up and down and the light of the moon was shimmering on the water. It gradually moved overhead and shone a beam of light down over me and I could feel it's healing energy.

A few days later, whilst in my canoe, a pile of money appeared on the floor in front of me, I felt that some money was going to come my way. In a way it did, as not long after, I managed to get a better deal on my telephone bill and I transferred some savings to a different savings account in order to accumulate a higher interest.

My friendly gorilla joined me at this point, he was holding a white cat which changed into a small white dog, then into a white kid goat. He handed it to me and I placed it on my lap. It changed back into the cat again. Animals are sent to give us comfort and the colour white for me, brings inner peace. I thanked them all for their kindness.

Ignato, had a humorous side to him as well. I had embarked on an on-line French course to keep my mind active during my retirement. I had always liked doing French at school and generally had got good grades, so I thought that this language was probably the best one to continuing learning. A few weeks later, I found myself in my rowing boat wearing a blue and white striped top, black trousers and a dark-coloured beret. My attire made me look like a French man! Ignato was having a bit of fun and it made me laugh.

Sadly, it was the last time that I felt Ignato around me. He had not given any indication that he was leaving me, nor any for-warning of a new spirit guide.

CHAPTER 12

Brian

I found myself in a rowing boat, instead of my familiar canoe when I next went into meditation. A man with a short brown beard appeared at the other end of it. He wore a three-cornered hat on his head and was surrounded by a cloak, casually, he removed his cloak and set it down in the bottom of the boat. I could see now that he wore black trousers and a type of jacket. He said, "I'm your man and I'm called Brian."

I asked him if he was a new spirit guide to which he replied," Yes, and I have come to help you with your mediumship." I thanked him, when he suddenly changed into an albino rabbit. I picked it up to give it a cuddle.

Brian took over the task of helping me before a service, as all the other guides had done before. Two days prior to a service at Blackpool, he sat in my place in the rowing boat, leaving me at the other end where my guests usually sit. He was wearing his familiar three-cornered hat and cloak, but that day there was a parrot standing on his left shoulder. In his right hand he held a long pole on the end of which was a lit lantern. Presumably he was lighting the way for me.

Next, I found myself lying face down on the ground, sunbathing on a mat. The sun was burning down and I could feel the heat on my back and then the sun changed into a brilliant white light which shone down over me, engulfing me. Although it was only April at the time, the weather had been very warm and I had been thinking about sitting outside to sunbathe. Brian must have known this.

The next day he visited again and was still sitting in my seat, a sign that he had taken over prior to the service that I was going to do. I saw a man putting up bunting over the two masts that had appeared in the rowing boat. This brightly coloured bunting stretched from the stern over the two masts to the bow.

The three of us began to clink our glasses of wine that had appeared out of the blue and Brian said, "You will do well my friend." From that time on I was always in a rowing boat and not in a canoe during my meditations with Brian.

I felt I had done well at the service. A lady came up to me afterwards and told me that she had enjoyed it very much even though she didn't get a message. A man also approached and thanked me for his message, he said he could take everything that I had said, but couldn't take a link to Spain at the time, however, he wanted to let me know that he had remembered that his son was going to Spain the following week.

I find that people don't always remember things, when I'm giving them a message and I have to admit that sometimes when I'm receiving a message, I've given a "No", only later realising it was in fact correct, proving that the medium was right after all. It's difficult to recall information when lots of names, places and dates are being given by the medium in quick succession. Sometimes, I've woken up in the middle of the night and had a "Eureka" moment when it has suddenly dawned on me what or who the medium was talking about. Indeed, I've sometimes had phone calls from sitters to whom I have given a reading, telling me about something that they couldn't take at the time.

Sometimes, people genuinely don't know and need to ask a relative about it, which is good proof in a way. I've had people approach me the next time they see me, to tell me that their mother or someone else has confirmed what I had told them.

The next day, after the Service, I was back in my rowing boat being handed a trophy rather like a football trophy with red, blue and white ribbons tied to the handles. The colour red for me means love and mental strength, blue signifies healing and white, inner peace. All gratefully received.

As usual, other people still visited me, as well as my guide, Brian. One day a man in full armour appeared in my boat. He grew taller and taller. I politely asked him to take a seat, which he did and enquired why he was wearing armour, "To protect you." He replied. I knew why he had come; I was being constantly patronised by a certain person and was glad that the spirits were there to help me. That person has since started to show me more kindness.

The meditation ended on a lighter note when I saw a violet flower rising from my crown chakra having got eyes, a nose and mouth. It began to blow its nose and dab its eyes, making me laugh because I had a cold at the time. The spirit world doesn't miss a thing!

Brian visited shortly afterwards, I didn't see him at first. Instead, I saw a lady dressed in a long white frilly dress, typical of the 1700's fashion, she was seated at the other end of the rowing boat with a boy of about four or five years of age. He was very shy, keeping his head low and not making eye contact with me. He wore a hat, a bit like a bowler hat, (which I later saw on the 1700's clothes website, confirming it was a hat-style for a boy of that era). He held a stick with string dangling from the furthest end and was trying to fish with it.

I asked them who they were, it was then that Brian appeared wearing his splendid three-cornered hat. He introduced them as his wife and son. I asked if his son had passed over when he was young, he confirmed this and I realised they had been quite well-to-do people, judging by their smart clothes.

Sometime later, his eldest son, who must have been in his teens when he passed over, introduced himself. He was carefully guiding my rowing boat over a water-fall, through some boulders and out onto still water. He was showing me my life symbolically at that moment, there were so many sad things happening.

He came again the next day, using a pole to guide the boat. I was about four years old and I was sitting in my seat dressed in clothes from the 1700's. He told me that I had been his sister, which would have made me Brian's daughter.

Apparently, we are often connected in some way to our guides, sometimes having been related to them as I was in this case, or we may have been someone who helped them in a previous life.

A few days later, another man wearing clothes and a hat, similar in style to those of Brian, appeared reading from a scroll which was being held by someone. He was quite animated and moved his arms around emphasising the words as he was reading. I felt perhaps this was a lesson for me when public speaking, instead of standing there like a statue and not moving much, it would be far more interesting for the congregation, if I moved about a bit more and gesticulated at the same time.

Prior to platform work, I had only ever given lectures at university or talks and presentations during my career and they often involved working with overhead projectors, pointing out important items out on the screen. Platform work is quite different, there are no visual aids to use, just the medium standing there in front of the congregation and so this man's advice was quite useful to know.

The sides of the boat rose and became very high, Brian knew that I had understood. Men appeared either side of the boat drinking wine and celebrating. They must be a boozy lot in the spirit world!

A meditation a few days later, left me feeling grateful to the spirit world. A man in a black suit and top hat was sitting in my seat in the rowing boat and began to row me to the gap in the mountains, surrounding the lagoon. A familiar place where I had been many times before.

White light came down and engulfed us. I asked for healing for my friend Joan, who was being nursed in intensive care, having fallen down a ravine and I saw her surrounded by white light. I also asked for healing for my sister's partner, Frank who was suffering from cancer and was seriously ill after having had a major operation, I saw white light surrounding him too. Thankfully, they both recovered and are still with us as I write this.

Spirits are always there to help and I needed their help when I had to go for an MRI scan, I had been suffering from a persistent sore throat, cough and a hoarse voice for many months and had been referred to a consultant who had organised a scan. I am a bit claustrophobic and knew that during the procedure patients laid on a trolley which was slid into a tunnel. I was quite apprehensive and wondered if I would cope.

The day of the appointment soon arrived. I was shown into a cubicle to change and after I had got ready, I sat waiting for the nurse to take me through to the scanner, it was then that I saw the outline of a little girl skipping in the pattern on the floor. There wasn't actually a girl in the pattern, but the different shapes seemed to give this impression. To my surprise, each time I blinked the little girl's legs moved and the skipping rope moved slightly, as though I was watching a slowed down film which was being moved forward a frame at a time, each time I blinked.

I had seen this little girl skipping many times in my visions, when giving spiritual messages. She usually came to reassure people, when they were apprehensive about an appointment, basically, indicating to them that they would skip through it. There she was giving me the same advice. It boosted my confidence and sure enough I did "skip through it." I kept my eyes closed throughout the entire procedure and meditated, imagining that I was outside in the countryside, listening to the birds and watching the trees blowing in the wind. It didn't even feel like I was lying in a very narrow tunnel.

Unfortunately, a lady in the next room must have had claustrophobia too for I could hear her screaming, presumably the procedure had to be aborted, but it had obviously upset her, as I could hear loud sobbing. If only she had known to meditate and take herself somewhere else during the procedure.

A diagnosis was made for me, following the scan and the appropriate treatment given, making me feel a lot better. However, my cough had never given me any trouble during the services when I was on the platform, I would ask my guides to stop me from coughing beforehand and they obliged, but as soon as the services ended, I was back to coughing again.

Miriam, once told me that something similar had happened to her. She had had a very painful ankle and wondered if she would be able to stand up on the platform for the duration of a service. Apparently, she had felt no pain at all throughout the entire service, until it ended, when it came back again.

I have noticed that mediums have good days and bad days with their mediumship, it could be due to a variety of reasons; the health of the medium, whether they are tired, very concerned about something or grieving for someone who has passed, the energies in the room of course, can have an effect too as I've mentioned before.

I am no different and had been to an Open Circle and had given four messages; one good, one average, one poor and one not taken at all! Perhaps my illness had had an effect. It had left me quite low and I hoped at the next two services, I would improve drastically. In fact, I told Brian, my guide that if I didn't do well, I would give up platform mediumship altogether.

Brian must have heard my plea for when going into meditation before the service at Cleveley's, I could see rockets shooting out of my chakras! They left beautiful trails of smoke behind them, matching the colour of each chakra.

Once I had opened up to the spirit world, I found myself sitting in my rowing boat, Brian threw another rocket into the air, it sped off at great speed into the sky and disappeared. I felt this was a sign that I was rocketing forward with my mediumship and the next couple of services proved it.

After the first one, I meditated and rockets shot out of my chakras as they had done before. In my boat I could see a young boy dressed in a Scottish outfit standing at the other end holding a lantern. We were in the lagoon that I was so familiar with, heading out to sea.

Next thing I knew I was aboard a large ship with three masts and found myself operating the ship's wheel. I joined lots of other boats, some much bigger than mine. I felt I had been put with the "big boys."

Below on the deck, I could see a captain in an old-fashioned uniform blowing a long trumpet. Bunting was flying between the masts on the ship. I felt that the spirits were congratulating me for the service I had done at Blackpool. I asked if I would do well in Southport in two days' time. I heard Brian say, "You will, I promise."

After the service, a lady said she was very pleased with the service and her message and asked me for my business card to arrange a reading. During the following two meditations, I found myself in the ship with three masts and went shooting off into the sky. Always a good sign.

My next meditation however, was quite different, I was momentarily in the ship before finding myself in a car looking through the eyes of the person driving it. I felt I was a female in her twenties driving through a forest of fir trees that were ablaze. I could see the raging fire, the tall red flames licking the trees and smoke billowing out high up into the sky and I could also smell the acrid smoke which was filling the air. All of a sudden, a large burning tree crashed onto the bonnet of the car. Everything went black.

I wondered if I had been someone who had actually passed over in a forest fire. Not long after, terrific forest fires were reported in Australia and I felt I'd had a vision from a future event.

The ship with the three masts featured once again in my meditation. I was standing on the ship only a metre away from Brian's son who was steering it. I sensed that we were in a battle on the high seas and could see fire spreading across the ship. I felt that this was how Brian's son had passed over, during this battle.

Sadly, it was the last time that I saw Brian and his family. It was time to move on to another guide.

CHAPTER **13**

Malcolm

I was standing on the quayside in my next meditation, looking at the ship, there were no signs of the fire anymore. It was all intact, just as it had been before the battle, but I was wondering why I wasn't standing on it. The sails dropped down and the ship began to move steadily out of the harbour. I started shouting for them to come back for me. "Why have you left me here?" I shouted. No one answered, I couldn't hear a sound from the ship.

A fireball appeared in the sky and took my attention away from the boat and as I gazed at it, the fiery ball slowly came towards me, gradually transforming into a man, who floated gently down to stand in front of me. He was an older man in his late fifties or early sixties wearing a checked waistcoat under his jacket. He also wore a black top hat and held a walking stick in his right hand. I guessed from his attire that he was probably from the late 1800's or early 1900's.

He cut the silence declaring, "I'm Malcolm, your new spirit guide." I offered my hand, to shake hands with him, he placed the hook of his stick over his left arm, but instead of shaking my hand, he took out his pocket watch from a small pocket in his waist coat and placed it on the palm of his hand. I could see that it was round and gold-coloured, Malcolm pressed a catch on the side of it and the top sprung open. A light blue metal bird popped up. I commented that it was beautiful and as I said this, the metal bird took off in flight into the sky. Malcolm looked at me and said, "You will fly again." Presumably referring to my mediumship.

The next time I saw Malcolm was at an Open Circle that evening. During the short meditation, he put his rather large top hat on my head and I could feel it tipping over on my right ear and found it a little irritating. I walked up a path to a small hill and sat on a bench. Malcolm stood in front of me and I asked him to help me along my spiritual path.

He held out his left arm and a pigeon alighted upon it. He explained, "The homing pigeon will find his way home and you will find where you need to be." I still didn't know what I was meant to do with my mediumship, I felt as though I could do more than just being a platform medium, perhaps it will be revealed to me in time.

The next day, I was sitting in the conservatory looking at the roofs of the houses when I saw an aura of purple around the roof of one house, I'd never seen this phenomenon before. I felt that healing was being given to the household, unfortunately, I didn't know the occupants, so didn't know their circumstances.

When I looked at another roof it was surrounded by the colour red. Love and mental strength were being sent to them.

It was unusual that I saw these colours surrounding the roofs, but it reminded me that I don't just do platform mediumship, but also channel a lot of healing to people when I'm working at the Healing Centre and The Gentle Approach Charity Centre. Unfortunately, due to the coronavirus pandemic all the Healing Centres have had to close, to stop the spread of the infection, so I have only been able to send absent healing to friends and family.

Prior to the next service, I found myself in my rowing boat with a man who was standing at the front of the boat, holding a shining lantern. We were slowly going along a dark tunnel and I could just about make out the curvature of the brick wall overhead and see the dark water surrounding us below. As we approached the end of the tunnel, there was a pin point of brilliant white light, that became larger and larger as we drew closer.

I could make out a tall Angel all in white, with huge wings. The rowing boat moved into the bright light and I fused with it as I had done so many times before. It is as if the spirit world makes this happen, to give me a greater connection with them before a service. I was due to give a service at Fleetwood, three days later.

The next day, instead of being in my rowing boat, I found myself standing in a park. There were lots of people dressed in the clothes from the late 1800's, it was raining and they all had their umbrellas up to protect themselves from the fine rain drizzling down. One of these umbrellas rose high into the sky, an indication that my mediumship would fly higher. The service went well.

Two weeks later, I was at another spiritualist centre sat in the mediums' room about to give a service and on that occasion, things were quite different during my meditation.

I was walking up some wooden steps, out of a dark tunnel. A man dressed in clothing from the late 1800's, who I had never seen before was walking backwards in front of me holding a lantern, to help me to see where I was going.

At the top of the steps a brilliant white light shone, lighting up the exit to the tunnel. The man continued to walk backwards into the light and disappeared. I soon followed him becoming fused with the light too.

Again, the service went well. One lady was reduced to tears when her spirit father had left her at the end of the message, with a silver sprayed twig, it had been a very special memory for her. She thanked me afterwards for such an accurate message. Another man thanked me too, he said I was spot on and couldn't believe that I had mentioned his ornamental rock at home, with stuck on wobbly eyes!

The next day during meditation, I was standing at the back of a crowd of people dressed in Victorian type clothes, holding up umbrellas as there was fine rain coming down again. The sky was full of black clouds and everyone was looking up towards it. A carriage drawn by four horses appeared though these clouds and I could make out two footmen standing up at the back of it.

The carriage and four horses landed softly on the ground in front of us all. I made my way through the crowd and as I approached it, the doors of the carriage swung open, I saw myself stepping inside the carriage taking off into the air and disappearing. That afternoon, I was serving another spiritualist church. A lady came up to me afterwards and said that she had enjoyed it very much.

A spirit lady had come through advising a relative of the recipient to stop drinking so much beer. She had been quite a character when she was here on the earth plane and was no different now, for she advised him to drink sherry instead! Apparently, it had been her favourite tipple and clearly, she felt it was far better for him, than drinking beer. Spirits don't change in the spirit world and sometimes their advice isn't the healthiest.

The spirits who come forward show themselves as they looked when they were on the earth plane. A relative of one of the members of the congregation, came into my vision, I could see that he was a slim man with dark hair, the top few buttons of his shirt were undone showing a rather hairy chest. He let me know that he was a practical man by hammering nails into something that he was making.

The client recognised the description and agreed that he was quite a practical sort of man. The spirit went on to give further evidence, before giving the reason for coming through.

Sometimes I'm shown actual medical tests or investigations. I have to be careful what I tell the recipient in front of the congregation and choose my words carefully.

A week later, whilst in meditation, Malcolm visited me, I was sitting on a bench and I asked for upliftment because I was a bit down in the dumps. He immediately pointed his stick to the sky, there was a flash of light and I could see a cherub, a beautiful winged child hovering in the sky, gazing down at me and I felt tremendous love pouring over me. I am truly grateful for the Angels and spirits looking after me and of course, they help everyone else too, all you need to do is ask.

I continue to have insights into future events, although I don't receive much information. On one occasion, I was meditating at home when I heard a voice say, "More stabbings," I saw lots of police cars and ambulances parked on the street. There were also a lot of policemen at the scene.

The next day, 29th November 2019, Usman Khan, a convicted murderer who had been released from prison, was attending a prisoners' rehabilitation conference, to which he had been invited. He set about attacking people, killing three and injuring three others throughout his vicious knife attack.

Usman Khan fled the building and was chased by brave security staff onto London Bridge, they were armed with only fire extinguishers and one of them had grabbed a long fish bone which had been displayed on a wall in the conference centre.

He was apprehended by these men and despite the fact they were aware of a bomb strapped to his chest, they bravely kept him pinned to the ground. When the police arrived, he continued to threaten everyone and kept up the struggle to free himself. The police shot him dead, fearing that he would detonate the bomb and kill everyone. The bomb was found to be a hoax, but because of the quick actions of the security staff, no further people had been stabbed.

The spirit world is aware of the future and often allow these events to happen, they don't always interfere. Some things are just meant to be.

In late March, I was in meditation again when I saw Malcolm, my guide, a few metres ahead of me in open countryside. He politely doffed his top hat and walked away, swinging his walking stick.

A helicopter flew over his head and I remember thinking that there were no helicopters in the late 1800's. I continued to watch Malcolm walk away, wondering why he hadn't spoken to me, meanwhile, the helicopter landed on the grass behind me.

I turned around to see a young man, wearing army combat uniform and a maroon beret, running towards me. He stopped abruptly in front of me and stood to attention, giving a salute.

He said, "I'm here to serve you."

"Why?"

"I'm your new spirit guide,"

I was quite surprised but thanked him. He told me that he was called Andrew.

The maroon-coloured beret is proudly worn by soldiers of the parachute regiment, which commenced in 1941. I felt it was rather appropriate that he should arrive airborne.

CHAPTER **14**

Andrew

A couple of days later, I found myself sitting on a wooden bench during meditation. It was perched on top of a flat grassy hill overlooking a deep valley below and I could see a large village sprawled along its length.

I could feel activity around my head and my hair was moving slightly, a sign that healing was being given. My Grandpa was also around me, tightening my throat, when a helicopter came into view, I couldn't see anyone, but knew my new guide, Andrew was there. He flew by and disappeared.

The next day, I could see him parachuting down from the sky. I knew this was a training exercise taking place on an expansive piece of land somewhere. He landed gently onto the extremely muddy ground, where there were great ruts in the bare soil, he discarded his parachute and ran off to join his comrades. He also showed me his Dalmatian dog, who is now in spirit with him.

Later that week, it wasn't Andrew who parachuted out of the helicopter, but a man in a black suit wearing a trilby hat. After landing on the hill, he walked towards me carrying a brown suitcase and set it down on the grass to open it. As he lifted the lid, I could see lots of paper money arranged in tidy piles. He scooped up large handfuls and placed the money onto my lap. "For you," he said, then he added, "You deserve it." I thanked him. It wasn't long afterwards that I received two lump sums of money, which were due to me.

Two days later, I'm not sitting on my bench, but on a motor bike, wearing leathers and a crash helmet. I felt Andrew had been a motorbike rider and I was on his bike. I watched myself ride over a wooden bridge, through a shallow stream onto rough flat land, then up a very tall pointed mountain. I realised, this was a symbolic depiction of my life of late, there had been great sadness in the family and I had felt compelled to cancel a holiday with friends to be with my sister, in order to comfort her. My health had also been very poor, having had complications following surgery.

Happily, Andrew showed me a straight path down the mountain, a sign that it would be plain sailing in my life for a while. I was thankful to know that and indeed, life did calm down.

A week later, Andrew appeared again in combat gear and maroon beret. He was walking very carefully across a tight rope, trying not to over balance and fall off. It was quite like my life at the time, as the whole country was in lockdown because of the coronavirus pandemic and I was fearful that I would catch the virus and be quite ill with it, because I suffer with a bad chest. Andrew was letting me know he was aware of the situation.

The scene changed and I saw him walking down some stone steps, attached to the outside of a stone building. A few metres ahead of him, on his right was a wooden door, which he opened. Inside, I could see a large room, down the middle of which was a long wooden table and other Para's were sat around it, busy chatting to one another. I felt that I was being shown a snapshot of his life.

He proceeded to show me snapshots of what was to come on the earth plane too. A man dressed in a smart black suit and top hot with a ginger-coloured beard, looking very much like a funeral director, walked stiffly to and fro, in front of me. I wondered why I was being shown this, but I didn't have to wait long, for I could see row upon row of coffins being pushed along on trolleys by men in black suits. I was quite shocked as more and more rows of coffins came into view. The rows of coffins went on and on....

We were three weeks into the lockdown and I believe I had just had a glimpse of the vast numbers of people who would pass over from this terrible coronavirus. It was very disturbing indeed.

A month later, we were still in lockdown, I had decided to go for my daily walk, and took the direction of the main street through my village for a change. I became quite emotional; it was almost deserted, the hustle and bustle had gone, the cheery greetings and chatter had fallen silent. There was only a couple of people on the pavement keeping their distance from each other and just a few of cars on the road. The main road through the village was usually very busy, but that day, I was able to cross the road at will, it's been many years since anyone could cross that road, without having to wait at the pedestrian crossing, for the traffic to stop.

On returning home, I meditated and found myself on the bench which seemed to be where I'm placed now that Andrew is my guide. It made sense being high up on a hill with a deep valley below, because he often appeared in an aeroplane or a helicopter.

I was reading a newspaper and relaxing on the bench, when I found myself taking off in flight. It was so sudden, that I didn't have time to fold my newspaper and tuck it under my arm. I objected, "Hang on," I shouted. Although annoyed, I managed to fold the newspaper in flight and safely tucked it under my arm. I flew over the village in the valley and could see traffic and pedestrians on the streets.

The next thing I knew, I was standing on a pavement watching a mayor, dressed in his long robe and wearing his chain of office, walk down the middle of the road. There was no traffic now and I wondered why he was doing this, when I noticed a procession of brightly coloured floats following a little distance behind him. Lots of people were lining the streets then and I could hear them laughing and chattering, enjoying the spectacle and as the procession came nearer, I could hear the music blaring out from the floats.

I was whisked away at this point and found myself looking down onto a street from the 1930's. Lots of people were rushing about involved in their daily business and old-fashioned cars were darting here and there in a rush to get somewhere.

I asked Andrew, "Why are you showing me this?"

I heard his voice say, "Showing you that life goes on."

Life indeed did go on as he had just shown me in a glimpse of life during the depression in the 1930's, when the country's economy was on its knees. Andrew was letting me know that even during these tough times that we find ourselves in now, life goes on and can only get better.

My eldest sister rang me a few days later, she is quite sceptical about spirit relatives being able to connect with people on the earth plane. She has admitted though that she has never had a psychic event in her entire life and I can understand her scepticism.

However, today it all changed.

To understand Meryl's story, I need to give some background: There was a popstar in our family. His name was Trevor Gordon and together with Graham Bonnet another musician, they called themselves "The Marbles." They were the backing group to the famous Bee Gees' first album and had several hits of their own in Australia, where they lived, but made it to number five in the UK charts with "Only One Woman," in

1968. My sisters and I had seen him only once before he moved to Australia.

Meryl's strange experience happened on 5th May 2020, when out of the blue, she was sent a link from You-Tube of The Marbles singing "Only One Woman". She told me that she was flabbergasted. Unbeknown to Meryl at the time, Trevor's birthday had also been on 5th May.

Meryl enjoys music and a few days earlier she had ordered an electronic keyboard. She had had one before, but as it was old, she had given it to one of her grandchildren.

Perhaps being a relative of Trevor, musical too, as well as having ordered a keyboard, it was the link Trevor needed to connect to Meryl in this way. Maybe he wanted to be remembered on his birthday.

The next day, I was sitting on my bench on the hill in meditation. I asked Trevor to come and visit me. I didn't expect anything to happen and was quite surprised when a young man, with shoulder length dark curly hair, suddenly stood in front of me. He looked very like Trevor and was wearing a long black coat with a large collar and lapels and proceeded to take off his brown leather gloves. I was quite amazed to see him, he didn't say anything however, before disappearing. I sang Happy Birthday to him, I hope he enjoyed it!

When I go into meditation, I never know what is going to happen and nearly a week later, I experienced something a bit different. I was aware of a naked baby rise out of my crown chakra. It was in a sitting position and at such an angle that I couldn't determine its gender. I wasn't in the dark for long, for I was shown a little boy clothed in blue jeans and a white t-shirt. Four months later, my daughter gave birth to a baby boy.

The meditation didn't end there, I saw a parade of Girl Guides, there were dozens of them, holding flags and walking down a street. "Put the flags out," came to my mind, which was quite significant, the coronavirus lockdown restrictions were being eased, much to everyone's relief.

My meditations vary a great deal and can be either connected to past, present or future events. During my next one, I found myself back on my bench overlooking the valley below, when a parachute high in the sky came into view. It descended and a man landed to the side of me. I noticed that it wasn't my spirit guide, but someone dressed in army uniform whom I had never seen before.

The man was carrying a small brown suitcase, typical of the 1940's era. He set it down in front of me and proceeded to open it. There were lots of papers inside and on the top piece of paper, I could read the title: "The Will," and the rest of the page was covered with typed words. I later learnt that my friend had been making his will.

I asked if I would do well at the next service. Unfortunately, I hadn't done any platform mediumship for several months due to the restrictions of the covid pandemic. Meeting in large numbers had been no longer permitted in order to stop the transmission of the disease from one person to another. I was a little apprehensive in case I had gone a little rusty with my mediumship.

I was sitting on my bench as usual, when a biplane displaying the RAF symbol on its side, started to fly past in front of me. I tried to have a good look to see who was in the plane, but couldn't see anyone properly. As it passed by, I caught sight of what looked like a long advertising streamer attached to the back of the plane, merrily waving in the wind. It said, "We will help you," of course, I knew they would, but I always seem to need a bit of reassurance. They were definitely there helping me, for the service went well.

Some days I can meditate and receive nothing from spirit, but that day was rather special. I was sitting on my bench reading a newspaper and on the right-hand page was a picture of an elderly lady, wearing a long black coat and a black hat which was rounded on top, with a small turned-up brim. The newspaper suddenly vanished and the lady in the newspaper was standing next to me. I asked her who she was. She replied, "Great Aunt Mary."

I have to say that at that moment, I couldn't recall a Great Aunt Mary, so went on to ask her why she had come. She said, "You need some comfort." I thanked her and could feel healing energy around my head and a slight movement of my hair.

After the meditation, I began to wonder who she was and remembered an old lady visiting our house once when I was quite young. My father had called her Aunt Mary. I had studied my ancestral tree several years earlier and decided to search through my notes. Sure enough, my Great Aunt Mary had been my Grandma's sister on my father's side. It was so lovely to see her and for her to come and give me healing.

It was quite appropriate for her to visit me at this time too, my lawn mower and television had both given up the ghost (pardon the pun) and I had dropped my mobile phone on concrete, resulting in huge cracks on its face, rather like a spider's web. Not a good week for me, but thankfully, Great Aunt Mary had cheered me up.

My next meditation was completely different however and gave me a glimpse into the future. Sitting on my bench on the hill, I could see a black cloud and flames rising up from a house below in the valley. Sadly, the next day it was reported on the news, that there had been an horrific house fire, a mother and her three children had lost their lives.

I had been asking spirit for a chance to do some more one-to-one readings, as I had not done any mediumship for six months. That same day, I had a phone call from a spiritualist church asking me if I would do some spiritual readings. Of course, I readily accepted.

The readings went well; one poor lady had lost a close relative a few months before, from the coronavirus, he had come through with quite a laid-back attitude, which was how he had been when he was here on the earth plane. He had visited because he wanted his relative to be more care-free, like him and to stop being so unhappy.

Her grandmother appeared who I identified, I described her and could see that she liked to sing whilst dusting and also enjoyed dancing and she wanted the client to enjoy herself too. Her grandfather joined me and said much the same thing. The sitter was tearful during the reading, but was grateful for her relatives coming through, especially the one who had been quite close to her and confessed that she had been consumed with grief since losing him. She realised that she must move on and start to go out and enjoy herself more.

When meditating later that day, a plane flew by with a long tail of balloons behind it! No doubt, Andrew had something to do with it and was celebrating for me.

Around this time, I had been sent information about a psychic detection course for missing people, to take place via zoom. The teacher and the students were from all around the world: USA, Norway, France, Australia, England and also Sweden. The course was welcome as nothing was happening in the churches as yet, due to the pandemic restrictions and the Open Circles had been cancelled too.

I had never done mediumship on-line before and wasn't sure if I could link into murder scenes on maps, photos of murderers or their victims from looking at a screen.

On opening up before the course, there were darts shooting out of every chakra, the colour of their feathers corresponding to the colour of each chakra. A toy helicopter went by, quite appropriate as my granddaughter and I had made an aeroplane from Lego bricks the day before. Andrew, my guide must have been around us at that time.

I asked Andrew, the reason for the darts. Immediately, a dart board came into view and I saw a person throwing darts. He said, "Have a stab at it." I'm glad I did register for the course, as I learnt many things, most notably, that it is in fact possible to locate where murders took place on a map and to link into a picture of someone to "see" events of their murder or to "see" through the eyes of a killer and to feel not only the emotions of the victim but those of the murderer too. It is also possible to give the names of these people, if not the full first name or the surname, then at least the first initial and this is all feasible via a computer screen.

Generally, we studied new and old cases of murder; stabbings, shootings and drownings, as well as cases of arson and death by drugs. Most of these murders had been solved and the perpetrators had successfully been brought to court and sentenced appropriately.

Sometimes I could "see" a victim being shot or stabbed in my vision where I was an observer during these events and so felt no pain or anguish. I could also "see" the surroundings and could determine if the murder had taken place inside, perhaps in the lounge or bathroom, or outside, either in the woods or by a river.

Of course, we didn't manage to obtain all the information individually, we would be very much in demand if we could have done that, but between us we often went a long way to solving many of the cases, including which country or town in the world it had taken place. It was a good course and I learnt many things.

The number of coronavirus victims had been growing again and the government had decided that the country should go into a stricter lockdown. Everything except essential shops and services were closed and we were only allowed to mix with one other family, forming a bubble, if we lived on our own.

Meryl, my sister and I had decided to communicate via Skype, essentially a video call, which we did three times a week. That day whilst we were talking, I could smell dog-breath, I have known several dogs and at first couldn't discern which spirit dog it was until I smelt disinfectant, Izal to be precise.

Meryl was given a dog called Laddie, when she was about ten years old. In those days, we lived in a fairly rural area and dogs were allowed out on their own. Laddie loved it when the farmers spread cow manure on the fields in spring and had a great time rolling in it. He would become plastered in the foul-smelling dung and would eventually make his way home.

He used to give one bark when he arrived at the front door and someone would let him in. if it was my Mum who found him in this state, she would put him in the garage until we children arrived home from school. Our first job was to bath him with diluted Izal; a strong awful-smelling disinfectant.

I have never forgotten that pungent smell and smelling it again made me realize that Laddie's spirit had come around me, whilst I was talking with his owner. It is always really nice to have a visit from the spirits, whether it is a person or an animal.

Whilst watching television one night, I could suddenly smell cowcake, food that we used to give to the milking cows, it was mixed in with many other ingredients and had a lovely liquorice smell, the horses loved it too.

As I was thinking about this, Silver, my horse from my childhood came into my mind's eye. She was my first pony, a Welsh Mountain mature mare, the matriarch of the herd. We had a tremendous bond between us and complete trust. She would allow me to pet her young foals even when they were first born, whereas everyone else had to be wary, as she would swing around ready to kick them, if they ventured too close.

I feel she came around me that day to give me comfort and remind me of the happy times we had together. Unfortunately, we were still in lockdown due to the coronavirus. I was only allowed to see my daughter and family who thankfully live quite close, non-essential shops remained closed and none of my clubs or groups were operating.

I really appreciated her visit, it made me think of happier times, when I used to ride her accompanied by my sister, who rode a gelding, called Prince. Sometimes we would saddle them up near to milking time to go and fetch the cows, who were often in a field up to half a mile away. On these occasions we would pretend to be cowboys rounding up the cattle. It was great fun.

To stem the boredom around this time, I started to do telephone readings, either by Whatsapp video calls or by telephone call. At first, I didn't know if I could link in to someone who I had never met on the other end of a phone and speaking to other mediums who had never tried it before, they were a bit apprehensive at first too.

I tried it out on a friend who I didn't see very often and so didn't know much about her. The reading went well and consequently I continued asking people to give my mobile number to anyone who was interested in having a reading. Luckily, I had a steady stream of clients, it helped to pass the time during lockdown.

Sometimes, whilst I was meditating prior to a telephone call, the sitter's spirit relatives were often so eager to come through that they presented themselves to me before I had even spoken to the sitter and would begin to tell me all about themselves, describing events that had happened, giving significant dates and many other things.

It was incredible that these spirits came before I had even spoken to the sitter, who often I had never even met before and only knew their first name and telephone number! It proves without any doubt at all, that spirit people are always very eager to connect with their loved ones and friends, here on the earth plane.

A few days later, shortly after the first telephone reading to my friend, I remember going into meditation finding myself sitting on my bench again, reading a newspaper, when I became aware of a very tall shadow figure on my left-hand side. I was a bit taken aback at first, but could sense my Grandpa around me, tightening my throat giving me reassurance that everything was OK. The shadowy figure was more than two and a half metres tall and I realized it was an Angel. The Angel said, "Come with me." We walked side by side through a wood into a clearing where a rocket shot off into the sky.

"This is you." The angel said, turning to me.

"So, my mediumship is going to take off?"

"With bells on!" I was surprised to hear that expression coming from an angel.

I found myself back on the bench again reading the newspaper when a small animal started climbing up it. I didn't know if it was a vole or a shrew, I asked, "What is it?" A voice said, "It doesn't matter what it is as long as you care for them all." Indeed, I do, for I have always loved animals.

In another meditation that week, I saw a lady in her seventies, wearing a black coat and hat, she looked very much like my identical twin of the triplets, as I was thinking this, a voice said," It's you."

The next day, I started to become ill with laryngitis, which developed into a nasty chest infection.

I could barely sleep at night for all the coughing and consequently had no energy in the day time. I went to have a covid test to rule out having contracted the disease. Thankfully, the test came back negative and I eventually got better after taking a course of strong antibiotics.

I felt that I had seen myself in my seventies because they were trying to reassure me that I would survive my illness and get better and presumably not die of the covid disease either, but would live for many more years to come. Only time will tell if this is true of course.

It was now January 2021 and very cold, in fact the temperature was dropping to minus three degrees centigrade at night and didn't get much higher in the day time. I have always suffered with the cold and Andrew, my guide must have been all too aware of it, for in my next meditation he flew by in his old-fashioned aeroplane and dropped a rectangular-shaped present in front of me. It was nicely gift-wrapped and tied with a red ribbon finished off with a perfect bow.

I got off my bench and opened it. Inside the box was a Onesie, one of those all-in-one night garments. It was very unusual though, as it was made from real fur with a pink triangular piece of material inserted at the front. How thoughtful was that? Andrew was thinking of me trying to keep warm at night.

The spirits seem to know everything, for the next day, I meditated and although I found myself sitting on my bench overlooking the valley, there was no village sprawled along the bottom. It had completely disappeared leaving a black area where it had once been.

I asked, "Where has it gone?"

"It will return." I heard Andrew say.

It did return the next time that I meditated. I knew later that Andrew was letting me know that the spirit world had been well aware of the dam about to burst in Pakistan. For a few days later, a huge chunk of glacier had broken off into the river rupturing the dam, which in turn had flooded the valley below and several villages had been swept away. It was then that I understood why the village in the valley had been missing in my meditation.

My telephone readings continued and I felt that Andrew, my guide was acknowledging this when he flew past in his helicopter, lowering a scroll of paper, a metre or so long showing a list of names of all the messages and readings I had given since starting mediumship.

He then lowered a rectangular box tied with a red ribbon from a thin rope. It settled on the ground in front of me. I unwrapped it and inside was a toy monkey with cymbals attached to its hands. I stood it on the ground and it started walking all by itself and as it did so, its hands came together and the cymbals clashed making a noise. I felt I was being applauded for all my messages and readings.

Nearly a week later, I hadn't anymore bookings for telephone readings and felt a little despondent. He came again and showed me the scroll of paper. I reminded him that he had already shown that to me, at which point the scroll of paper grew longer and longer, until it stretched for miles all the way to the horizon.

The next day I took three bookings.

I am destined it seems from the length of that scroll, to carry on my mediumship for a long time to come. Who knows where my journey will take me in the future?

I feel I have come such a long way on my spiritual journey since that first service which Julie took me to, over seven years ago now, where for the first time I saw a medium working from the platform and was truly struck by his ability to connect with the spirit relatives and friends of the congregation.

Once the covid pandemic restrictions are lifted and we are all allowed to be free, to go where we please, I'm sure there will be more opportunities for me.

I am for ever grateful to those in the spirit world for their teachings, guidance, reassurance and encouragement, as well as for their healing.

Writing this book during the lockdown has definitely given me a purpose. I have been totally absorbed and the time has passed so quickly. It has kept me occupied during those long days and kept me sane too.

Some of my friends sadly, have suffered from depression and anxiety, not being able to visit loved ones nor see their friends.

Luckily, I have largely kept upbeat! I may not have been able to see friends and many of my family on the earth plane, but my family and friends in the spirit world have visited me regularly, cheering me up when I felt low, giving me advice and encouragement and helping me in my new ventures of telephone readings and connecting to murder cases. I am forever grateful to them all.

Epilogue

I have written this book with a view to helping others who have grown up experiencing weird and wonderful events such as premonitions, forebodings, unusual dreams, telepathy as well as actually seeing spirits and who don't fully understand what it's all about and don't know of anyone who can help them.

I have given an open and frank account of my journey so far, although everyone's journey is quite different, but remember your spirit guides are always there to guide you and for those who haven't had any spiritual experiences at all during their life, I hope after having read this book, you will have a better understanding of those who do.

My book has given an insight into the world of spirit and how to go about developing your "gift" either by going to classes at spiritualist churches, joining courses on-line or enlisting on courses at various venues across the country.

My best wishes go out to all of you, especially to those of you who decide to take that next step along their spiritual path.

About the Author

Viv was born in 1954, the second of triplet girls. She was brought up on the outskirts of Batley, near Leeds in West Yorkshire. She gained an honours degree in microbiology and became a Registered General Nurse at the old Liverpool Royal Infirmary. After marrying her husband in 1977, they went to live near Preston in Lancashire and had two lovely daughters.

Viv has had psychic events throughout her life, but didn't go on to develop her mediumship until she retired at the age of 59 years. She wishes to pass on her experiences to others who would like to develop their "gift", but not sure what it is all about and how to go about it.

Printed in Great Britain
by Amazon